# THE ART
# OF LISTENING:
# DEVELOPING
# MUSICAL PERCEPTION

# THE ART
## OF LISTENING:
## DEVELOPING
## MUSICAL PERCEPTION

**HOWARD BROFSKY**

QUEENS COLLEGE,
THE CITY UNIVERSITY OF NEW YORK

**JEANNE SHAPIRO BAMBERGER**

FOREWORD BY
ROGER SESSIONS

**HARPER & ROW, PUBLISHERS**

NEW YORK · EVANSTON · LONDON

Illustrations by *Virgil Burnett.*

**To our students**
whose wisdom and insightful
criticism have been an immeasurable
source of guidance and inspiration

# CONTENTS

## STRUCTURE: PROCESS AND DESIGN

## THE HISTORICAL CONTEXT

Contents

# PREFACE

The urgent need for a new approach to the teaching of an introductory music course led to the development of our own materials for this course. Several years of seemingly continuous discussion of goals and means, followed by a critical analysis of the results as we have observed them and discussed them with our students, brought forth the book in its present form.

During the long hours devoted to selecting examples as well as to the actual writing of the text, each of us used the other as sounding board, critic, and mentor; thus no part of the book is the sole effort of either one of us. We hope that those who use the book will learn as much from it as we have learned in creating it.

Howard Brofsky
Jeanne Shapiro Bamberger

# FOREWORD

This book can be of great value to the student or "layman" who is attracted to music and who seeks to gain from it all that it has to offer him. To be sure, the reader will not be able to achieve his goal without effort; but it is not the authors of the book, but music itself, which demands this effort—an effort no greater and no less, after all, than that demanded by any of the other major arts.

The quotation from Stravinsky that introduces Chapter 1 should be pondered and kept constantly in mind as a kind of premise underlying all that the student can learn from the book. *The Art of Listening* is presented by its authors against a background of a general course in humanities at The University of Chicago; and the book's value derives from the authors' firm conviction that understanding of music, on any level whatever, is to be found only in music itself, and in a direct awareness of music rather than information about it. Much of the value of the book therefore stems to a large extent from its earlier portions, in which the reader is shown, through simple and effective steps, how such direct awareness can be cultivated. The authors have organized their material clearly and well, with a view to the reader's experience; they introduce each element first in its most immediately apprehensible form and follow this directly by illustrations of its application in a larger context. In doing so, material is drawn from a large variety of sources in such a manner, one would expect, as to stimulate the reader's curiosity and make him aware of the fact that the horizons of music are indeed very broad. The authors, by repeated emphasis, make clear the fact, often neglected, that these so-called elements of music must in no way be considered as independent of each other; they are facets of a whole that is indivisible by its very nature.

The authors also—without undue insistence but nevertheless very clearly—emphasize the importance of genuine involvement on the part of anyone who is drawn toward music, whatever the motive or the nature of this involvement may be. Such involvement is taken for granted by virtually everyone in literature and the visual arts, but is much less generally understood in music. No one could be very seriously regarded as a lover or connoisseur of poetry if his experience of poetry were limited to occasional cursory readings which did not include his lingering over the poem and savoring every detail to the full. The same quality of "savoring" is considered intrinsic to an appreciation of the visual arts. The problem with music, however, lies in the impermanence which constitutes its very nature. Far more than any art, its whole existence is in the realm of time, to which it gives shape and content. Like time, music passes, and its regulated flow is of the very essence. One cannot linger over music and enjoy its flavor to the full without, on the one hand, playing or singing it, or, on the other, listening to it attentively and repeatedly, and thus becoming aware of its movement in detail.

The authors (wisely, I believe) have left for the last chapters the section of the book whose function is solely to provide information, historical and otherwise. This information is provided in summary fashion, and ample indications are given as to where additional factual material can be found if desired. That such information should be offered is natural, if only to satisfy the curiosity of the reader. The reader will in the course of the book have become acquainted with a wide variety of music and may well have become curious as to the sources of and reasons for this variety. However, today probably as never before—and probably above all in colleges and universities—it needs to be tirelessly emphasized that music, like every other art, has existence and values of its own, quite distinct from its history, its ethnology, or its theory. It is these values which must be paramount if music is to be understood in any sense at all. The authors of *The Art of Listening* have, I believe, understood this point exceptionally well. Here too their aim is to stimulate the student's powers of observation and independent judgment. While starting with categorical distinctions of a conventional, and therefore convenient, nature, they quickly take pains to point out the looseness and inadequacy of these distinctions and the richness and variety and freedom of invention which lies beneath and ultimately remains quite independent of them.

**Roger Sessions**

*Cambridge, Mass.*
*November, 1968*

# Means and Possibilities

*Medieval Music Manuscript*
(The Pierpont Morgan Library, New York)

# INTRODUCTION *1*

> . . . verbal dialectic is powerless to define
> musical dialectic in its totality.
>
> STRAVINSKY[1]

This book has developed from the introductory
humanities course offered at The University of
Chicago. There were no prerequisites for the
course. Neither an ability to read music nor any
extensive familiarity with it was required. Through
encouraging an exchange among students and
between students and instructor, we tried to discover the paths through which students become
actively involved with music. The primary emphasis
both in our classes and in the book is on experience itself rather than on facts about music, terminology, or techniques.

In using this book and the accompanying records,
we ask you first to consider your own experience
with a given example, then to try to determine what
in the music has contributed to this experience,
and finally to return once more to your own experience in the light of your more conscious awareness

[1]Igor Stravinsky, *Poetics of Music,* Harvard, Cambridge, Mass.,
1947, p. 123.

of what has stimulated it. We insist, then, that the learning process be an active one, one in which you are, from the beginning, personally involved, questioning, and critical.

Following the cue of our students, we begin with that aspect of music which seems most immediately accessible: its purely sensuous impression. We examine a variety of possibilities for making and combining sounds in the works of different composers (Chapter 2). Our initial isolation of certain aspects of sound leads to a discussion of how these aspects are combined and interrelated in a more complex fashion, which, in turn, leads to another dimension: rhythmic organization (Chapter 3).

You will discover, for instance, the notion of measured time—the beat and the grouping of beats into larger units of time. (We have struggled against the language used to describe time; for example, time is spoken of as if it consisted of spatial entities—time is "larger" or "longer"—and this verbal habit influences our ability to experience time as a series of events.) From here we go on to combine and interrelate other factors. We ask you to consider the relative duration of whole musical gestures and how these varying durations influence your experience of specific works. But it becomes necessary to step back from these broader considerations to isolate elements once again, this time in order to consider pitch and melodic organization (Chapter 4).

With our next concerns, larger organizational possibilities—return, repetition, motivic development (Chapter 5)—and harmony (Chapter 6)—we begin to move outward from the details of specific and rather isolated pitch relationships to larger configurations. The course will reach its culmination when you are able to perceive rhythmic, melodic, and harmonic aspects not as isolated factors but as parts of an inseparable whole, combining and influencing one another to generate the events, motion, and process of a unique work. At this moment we come to the notion of *function* (Chapter 7), that is, to the dramatic transformations of musical material which generate, on the one hand, changes in affect (stability, instability, tension, repose) and at the same time structure (statement, transition, development, ending).

Having begun, then, with your response to an immediately perceptible aspect of music—sound relationships—our analytic process leads to greater and greater specificity. Through a growing awareness of specific musical means we move toward more complete perception of, and response to, the total piece of music which those means generate. The excitement you feel in response to a significant detail in a small excerpt develops into the possibility for fuller participation in a complete work.

Now let us consider the recorded material itself. You will notice that the excerpts become longer as we move from isolated aspects of music toward the total experience of a work. Thus, in the earlier demonstrations of texture, rhythmic relationships, or pitch relationships, you will find shorter excerpts chosen to focus your attention on one particular element. Later, when we are concerned with structure, function, or style, the excerpts will grow longer until finally you are dealing with complete works. Obviously, this organization reflects in a practical fashion the process which we described above: the movement from the perception of isolated aspects toward the perception of these aspects as an inseparable whole, a specific work with its unique emotional impact.

With the goal of this kind of perception in mind,

we ask you from the beginning to listen carefully to each example, always with the appropriate section of the book in hand. Without the book, the musical examples will seem a strange and often meaningless hodgepodge. In many instances, you will be asked to hear very specific details. You will need to listen several times before you grasp aurally what has been described. On the other hand, some demonstrations—Fundamentals of Rhythm or Melodic Motion and Shape, for example—may seem overly simple, particularly to those of you who play an instrument. But while these demonstrations may seem rudimentary, they are fundamental to our later concerns. They provide a consistent base upon which to build by putting forth in as functional a manner as we are able the underlying, often unconscious, foundations on which your musical experience is based. For the less experienced listener these rudimentary demonstrations should serve as initial steps; for the more experienced listener they should provide an opportunity to organize and make conscious knowledge that may have been already acquired in a rather random fashion. The goal throughout the book is "developing musical perception."

You will notice, too, that the examples in any one demonstration are chosen from widely different periods (dates of composition are included whenever they are known). Thus, in addition to the overt reason for including an example, we have also the intention of gradually developing your awareness of and sensitivity to a wide range of musical styles. Indeed, you might find it revealing to take a group of examples which are juxtaposed because they are in some way the same and ask yourself, in the light of perhaps a 300-year time span separating their dates of composition, what makes each of them so different from the others.

Means and
Possibilities

We have often found that students develop a special taste for some composer or some period of music and may be annoyed because they are hearing only little bits of this music. This limitation obviously cannot be remedied within the framework given here, but the short pieces can serve to stimulate you to move out into the broader world of music.

Finally, in the last section of the book we consider directly the historical context of music. We have put off considering the significance of the historical moment in which a work is written for two reasons: (1) To grasp the characteristics of a particular composer's style or the style of a group of composers writing contemporaneously requires all the listening skill that you have been acquiring before you reach this section. (2) Historical significance can only be understood against the background of experience with music of all periods surrounding and including the one which might be our particular concern. Thus, both our direct and indirect intentions must play a role in this final section. We do not attempt in our consideration of history to provide a short history of music or even a summary of all the features of different styles; rather we ask you to consider how an awareness of tradition and style influences your perception of individual works. We are concerned, then, with historical context as only *one* of the aspects contributing to your total involvement with a piece of music. The primary goal of this last section is to encourage you to listen to each piece of music *in its own terms*. This kind of listening requires an awareness of the terms—that is, of the style of the music. Remember, however, that the identification of a style, period, or composer ought not to be a substitute for actually listening to the unique events of each work.

At the end of most chapters you will find a section entitled Additional Materials. These sections should not be considered as "extra"; they are an integral part of the book. Sometimes they present various kinds of exercises which encourage you to "perform" actively, but most important, they recommend further listening through which you can extend your newly acquired musical perception outward from the excerpts in the demonstrations to longer musical examples—in many cases, to whole pieces. We have tried with these Additional Materials to show how various aspects of music actually function within the context of whole works. You are strongly urged to find recordings of the works recommended or refer back to the examples discussed if they have already been included in a demonstration. At the end of the book you will also find a section called Ancillary Reading which includes a number of definitions and various facts about music.

One of the greatest problems we have faced in preparing this book is that of the distortion which is necessarily introduced whenever some aspect of a total organism is isolated—whether that organism be a living thing or a piece of music. An examination of any one aspect of music immediately distorts your hearing of those pieces we have chosen as illustrations, since we are asking you to listen only to that one facet of the music and to leave out others which also contribute to the total effect.

While this problem cannot be entirely avoided, we have tried to overcome it in two ways: (1) by choosing examples in which the particular aspect of music under consideration is a significant factor in the total experience; and (2) by trying to keep in mind all the facets of a given moment in a

Means and
Possibilities

piece—such as rhythm, harmony, and melodic shape—as they influence the particular aspect which may be our temporary concern.

The problem is further complicated by the fact that any excerpt is only a moment in the total time span of the work, so that in our process of analysis we are not only slicing the music into its component parts but also slicing it vertically, so to speak, into bits of time. That music takes place in time and not statically in space is a constant problem in trying to describe its effect: as soon as we stop it to look or listen closely, we are distorting the significance of the work as a total organism.

There is a certain discomfort involved in this fracturing of what is a continuous, often immediate, emotional experience which one wishes kept inviolable. However, we are operating under the belief that a degree of analysis and objective scrutiny, both of the music and of the listener himself, will contribute, in time, to the intensity of such immediate and inviolable experiences.

One more problem must be added here; the distortion introduced by the words used to describe musical phenomena. Just as we urge you to consider your own responses to a given example first, so we urge you to search for words which will appropriately describe both your own response and the attributes of the music which have stimulated it. We have attempted to avoid all terminology which has been derived only from the vague, often inaccurate, assumptions of traditional usage. To describe what is a complex intellectual, emotional, and highly personal experience generated by an equally complex set of phenomena is a difficult task; we feel, however, that the effort can be a most important way of exploring the manifold dimensions of music itself.

Finally, we would like to emphasize that the book *tells* you very little; the valuable results will come from what you can discover yourself by actively studying the musical examples, using the book as a guide and mentor. The facts we give *about* music are only important when they are transformed into your live experience—and that you must have alone. "The really 'understanding' listener takes the music into his consciousness and remakes it, actually or in his imagination, for his own uses."[2]

[2] Roger Sessions, *The Musical Experience of Composer, Performer, Listener,* Princeton, Princeton, N.J., 1950, p. 97.

Means and
Possibilities

# Demonstration 1
## The Variety of Music
### (side 1)

We begin by listening to excerpts from a wide variety of music. Since music of some kind is a part of everyone's experience, this demonstration is certainly not an introduction to music; however, it should serve as an introductory inquiry into exactly *how* one listens to music and *what* one hears (and comprehends). All the examples but two appear again in subsequent demonstrations; at this point we include them simply to stimulate your own initial inquiry—to raise questions rather than to answer them. Later you may find it useful to turn back to this set of examples to compare your initial responses with your more experienced ones.

You will notice that the examples represent a wide range of music, both chronologically and geographically. As you listen, each piece will create an instantaneous impression, a unique "sound world"—a physical, emotional, intellectual, and cultural context. What in the music itself generates this unique experience?

I

| Example | Composer, Title | Date |
|---------|----------------|------|
| 1.1 | *Solea* (Flamenco) | |
| 1.2 | R. Newman, *Just One Smile* (performed by Blood, Sweat, and Tears) | 1968 |
| 1.3 | Stravinsky, *Le Sacre du printemps,* Danse sacrale | 1913 |
| 1.4 | Bach, *Concerto in D Minor for Harpsichord and Orchestra* | c. 1730 |

Listen only to the first four examples. It is unlikely that you would hear these four pieces together anywhere but in the artificial circumstances created by a book. Yet this juxtaposition will set in relief the striking differences among them—differences not only in your immediate experience of the music but also in the musical means used in the pieces to generate these differences. Finding words to express them will be difficult, yet certain aspects of each work are evident at once. What about instrumentation, rhythm (each has a strong beat, but how do they differ rhythmically?), and melody? What other questions are raised by juxtaposing these pieces? What constitutes their variety?

II

| Example | Composer, Title | Date |
|---------|-----------------|------|
| 1.5 | *Veni Creator Spiritus* (Gregorian Chant) | Middle Ages |
| 1.6 | Schoenberg, *Herzgewächse* | 1911 |
| 1.7 | Haydn, *Symphony 99*, minuet | 1793 |
| 1.8 | Mahler, *Symphony 1*, second movement | 1888 |

Examples 1.5 and 1.6, a medieval chant and a twentieth-century song by Arnold Schoenberg, suggest the vast possibilities of music for voice. What diametrically different uses of pitch and time can you discover as you listen? Are the pieces in any way similar?

In comparison, the Haydn and Mahler examples, although their dates of composition are separated by nearly a hundred years, sound relatively similar; the excerpts are both dance movements from symphonies, and both belong to the same tradition. What musical attributes contribute to this sense of a common heritage?

Means and
Possibilities

| Example | Composer, Title | Date |
|---------|-----------------|------|
| 1.9 | Webern, *Five Pieces for Orchestra*, Opus 10, no. 2 | 1913 |
| 1.10 | Boulez, *Le Marteau sans maître* | 1955 |

Finally, two twentieth-century works by Anton Webern and Pierre Boulez are given. These pieces may sound very much alike to you, yet close listening will reveal striking differences between them. What fundamental questions do these last examples raise; what do you want to ask about them? Can you relate them to the earlier examples in any way? (Notice that the Webern piece was written only 25 years after the Mahler symphony movement and 42 years before the Boulez piece.)

To provoke more questions and perhaps to answer some it will be especially profitable to exchange ideas with others as you listen to these examples. Many of the aspects of music which will emerge from such discussions will become the particular concern of subsequent demonstrations. The purpose, then, of this initial plunge, is to stimulate your discovery of some of these manifold dimensions.

*Triumph of Eternity*
Chaumont tapestry panel, France, 1500–1510
(The Cleveland Museum of Art; gift
from various donors by exchange)

# SOUND RELATIONSHIPS 2

Demonstration 2

Sound

(side 1)

The examples in Demonstrations 2 and 3 and Exercise 1 have been chosen in order to focus your listening on the great variety of sound relationships which exist in music. Since the range of possible sound relationships is limited only by the capabilities of the available instruments or voices and by the imagination of the composer, the examples given are by no means all inclusive. Rather, they are intended to generate an increasing sensitivity to sounds and the ways in which they can be combined and interrelated.

The descriptive commentary for these and subsequent demonstrations should be used as a guide, not as a substitute for careful listening. Words about music are utilized here in order to serve two purposes: (1) to direct your attention to what *should* be heard, and (2) to describe what, in fact, you *have* heard. But note that both of these uses are part of the analytic process which functions as a middle phase between your initial experience with a work and later, your more complete experience of it. In the end, then, it is your hearing of the music itself which should teach, not the words about it.

The examples in Demonstration 2 were chosen to raise some initial questions about sound relationships; they are arranged to show the following sources of variety in sound:

1. The differences in density of sound when one (Group I), few (Groups II, III, and IV), or many (last two examples of Group V) instruments (or voices) are playing at a given moment.
2. The influence of the particular instrument or instruments playing on the effect of different densities.
3. The role the instruments (or voices) play in relation to one another—melody and accompaniment, two equal instruments, and so forth.

It is important to recognize that in the actual experience of music one does not separate these aspects of sound—that each of these and other factors, as well, create the total sound fabric of a given moment. Notice that the character and the particular sound of each example is rather different, even though some of the examples are grouped together because the same number of instruments is playing or the relation among instruments is the same. For example, as you listen, think about the aspects of music which make the experiences of Examples 2.1 and 2.2, 2.3 and 2.4, or 2.5 and 2.6 so different. It is also important to bear in mind that the examples are excerpts from larger works and that our ultimate goal is to apprehend the great variety of possible sound relationships as they contribute to the experience of a whole work with its own particular organization and effect.

Means and
Possibilities

16

I

| Example | Composer, Title | Date |
|---------|----------------|------|
| 2.1 | Varèse, *Density 21.5* | 1936 |
| 2.2 | Bach, *Partita 2,* gigue | c. 1720 |

The first two examples are played by one instrument alone. Notice, however, that the character and the particular sound of each example is rather different, due to the particular instrument playing as well as to a number of other factors.

II

| Example | Composer, Title | Date |
|---------|----------------|------|
| 2.3 | *Gaudete Populi* (Mozarabic Chant) | Middle Ages |
| 2.4 | Bach, *Concerto in D Minor for Harpsichord and Orchestra* | c. 1730 |

In these two examples there is again only one melody line, but now more than one voice or instrument is producing it. This is known as playing "in unison" and may involve a group of men all singing exactly the same pitches (Example 2.3), a group of men and women singing together, or a group of instruments (such as violins, violas, cellos, basses, harpsichord, as in Example 2.4) all playing the same melody but in different registers (higher and lower). Given this point of similarity between the two examples, why are they so different? (As one approach, try "keeping time" to each.)

III

In this group of excerpts the melody line is heard together with a minimal accompaniment—merely

| Example | Composer, Title | Date |
|---------|-----------------|------|
| 2.5 | Tamil Folk Song (India) (Notice that unison singing alternates with solo singing) | |
| 2.6 | Bach, *St. Matthew Passion*, recitative | 1729 |

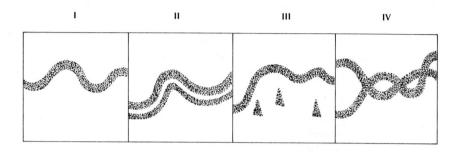

I       II       III       IV

drums (Example 2.5) or a few chords (Example 2.6). Notice that while your interest focuses primarily on the melody in these examples, the added element of accompaniment influences your perception of the melody, creating a more complex experience. Thus, it is not so much the number or kind of instruments playing, as the respective role of the parts in relation to one another that differentiates these examples from those in Group II above.

IV

| Example | Composer, Title | Date |
|---------|-----------------|------|
| 2.7 | Gibbons, *Fantasia a 2* | c. 1608 |
| 2.8 | Beethoven, *Trio*, Opus 11 | 1798 |
| 2.9 | Mozart, *Duo for Violin and Viola*, K. 424 | 1783 |

While Group III involved pieces with more than one instrument or voice, one part clearly predominated—that is, there was a clear foreground–background relationship. The examples in Group IV illustrate music for two parts each of *equal* importance. This means that a more complex sound fabric is created and thus the listener must follow not simply one predominant part, but rather sometimes one part, sometimes the other, and sometimes both as they vie with one another for the foreground role.

V

| Example | Composer, Title | Date |
|---------|-----------------|------|
| 2.10 | Caccini, Madrigal | 1602 |
| 2.11 | Schubert, *Die Schöne Müllerin*, Der Müller und der Bach (Notice that the accompaniment in the second part of the song becomes more active, thus drawing more attention to itself) | 1823 |
| 2.12 | Flamenco Dance Song | |
| 2.13 | Bartok, *Violin Concerto*, first movement | 1938 |
| 2.14 | Mahler, *Kindertotenlieder*, no. 2 | 1901–1903 |

In this last group of examples you will hear a single voice (or melody instrument) with an accompaniment that plays a more significant role than it did in the examples of Group III. Notice, however, that within this group, the density of sound varies from one example to the next according to the number and kind of instruments playing the accompaniment: from Example 2.10 (lute alone) and Example 2.11 (piano alone), all the way to the large orchestra of Examples 2.13 and 2.14.

## Demonstration 3
### Texture
### (side 2)

The examples in this demonstration have been chosen to illustrate further possibilities for varying the role of instruments or voices in relation to one another. This aspect of music is usually referred to as *texture*. As is so often the case with musical terminology, this term has been derived by analogy from other areas of experience. Reflecting the visual and tactile characteristics of fabric, "texture" as used in music is a function of the strands (or lines) of sound, and the relationships among them. Within this rubric it is useful to be able to speak of the texture of a piece in terms of such elements as density, activity, or its upper or lower parts.

You will undoubtedly notice other musical relationships in addition to texture contributing to the unique effect of each example in this demonstration. In preparation for our consideration of other aspects of music, question your experience of each work and try to discover, as well as differences in texture, what has stimulated the particular experience.

I

Listen again to Examples D2.11 and D2.14,[1] which illustrate melody with accompaniment. Despite

[1] The system of annotation for recorded musical examples throughout the text is as follows: "D" indicates "demonstration"; "E" indicates "exercise." Thus D2.11 refers to Example 11 in Demonstration 2; E2.11 would be Example 11 in Exercise 2. AM indicates the "additional materials" section given at the end of the chapter.

Means and
Possibilities

their textural similarity, they differ in several ways:

| Schubert | Mahler |
|---|---|
| Voice and piano | Voice and large orchestra |
| Intimate; appropriate for a "house concert" or small performance hall | Public; appropriate for a large concert hall |
| The singer plays a clearly predominant role; the piano is always in the background | The singer's voice is always heard, but the orchestra plays a significant role in creating the sound atmosphere |

## II

| Example | Composer, Title | Date |
|---|---|---|
| 3.1 | Chopin, *Prelude*, Opus 28, no. 4 | 1838 |
| 3.2 | Chopin, *Prelude*, Opus 28, no. 6 | 1838 |
| 3.3 | Chopin, *Prelude*, Opus 28, no. 20 | 1838 |
| 3.4 | Chopin, *Prelude*, Opus 28, no. 5 | 1838 |

The four short pieces in this group are all for piano alone; however, they illustrate four rather different kinds of relationships resulting from the presence or absence of a melody line, or the role of the melody within the sound fabric. Examples 3.1 and 3.2 have a clear melody with subordinate accompaniment, and in each case the accompaniment has a consistent character of its own. Notice, however, that the melody in Example 3.1 is in the highest part of the texture while in Example 3.2 it is primarily in the lowest part. For a variety of reasons, one tends to focus more readily on the uppermost part of a musical texture. Therefore, tension might be generated when the melody is in one of the lower parts (thus giving that part the

Sound
Relationships

21

foreground role), or when the upper part shares the foreground role with other parts. How do differences in the melodies, themselves, contribute to the difference in the total effect?

In Example 3.3, the melody is the upper "layer" of a series of chords; that is, all of the parts move along together and thus the accompaniment has no distinguishable character of its own. In Example 3.4, there is hardly a melody at all. What do you listen to in this piece?

## III

| Example | Composer, Title | Date |
|---------|-----------------|------|
| 3.5 | Bach, *St. Matthew Passion*, chorale | 1729 |
| 3.6 | Bach, *St. John Passion*, chorus | c. 1723 |
| 3.7 | Morley, *O Grief, e'en on the Bud* (madrigal) | c. 1590 |
| 3.8 | *Desconforté ai esté / Amas qui m'a* (motet) | 13th century |
| 3.9 | Gibbons, *The Silver Swan* | 1612 |

Examples 3.5 and 3.6 have been grouped together because they both involve a large chorus (several

**3.5** *"the parts generally move together"*     **3.6** *"the parts are independent"*

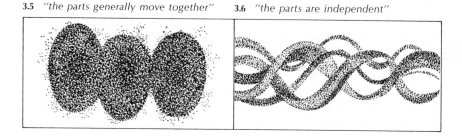

people singing each part), in contrast to Examples 3.7 and 3.8, which involve only a small group of singers (one person on a part). The comparison here, in terms of the "social" function of the music,

Means and
Possibilities

22

is similar to that between the Schubert and Mahler songs, insofar as Example 3.7 (and probably 3.8 as well) would have been performed at home or at private court concerts, whereas Examples 3.5 and

**3.7, 3.8** *"a small group of singers (one person on a part)"*

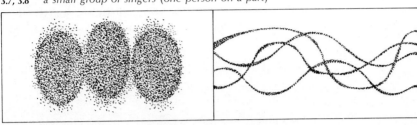

3.6 were written for a service in a large church. On the other hand, in terms of the activity of the texture, Examples 3.5 and 3.7 are similar in that all the parts generally move together (notice the striking effect when they do not), whereas in Examples 3.6 and 3.8 the parts are rhythmically and melodically independent. Example 3.9 illustrates the textural flux frequently found in music, utilizing both textures shown in the previous pairs of examples.

It will be observed that none of these pieces is a completely "pure" example of a particular kind of texture—such examples usually exist in textbooks, but rarely, if at all, in live music. The listener will notice, for example, that in Example 3.5 the lower parts occasionally move somewhat independently of the top part, although the dominant textural character is nonetheless one in which all the parts move together. Furthermore, in Example 3.8, where there is the greatest independence of the parts, the three lines still come together at certain points.

## IV

This group of examples illustrates some of the possible roles a singer may play in relation to the

Sound
Relationships

| Example | Composer, Title | Date |
|---|---|---|
| 3.10 | Verdi, *La Traviata,* "Libiamo ne' lieti calci" | 1853 |
| 3.11 | Mahler, *Songs of a Wayfarer,* no. 2 | 1883 |
| 3.12 | R. Strauss, *Salome,* final scene | 1905 |
| 3.13 | Boulez, *Le Marteau sans maître* | 1955 |

instrumental accompaniment. The progression within the group is as follows:

Example 3.10  The accompaniment is subordinate.

Example 3.11.  Larger orchestral forces and a more active texture begin to impinge on the singer's role as "leading lady."

Example 3.12.  The singer is almost enveloped by the orchestra.

Example 3.13.  The singer's voice becomes merely another color among the instruments—one among the many.

**3.10-3.13**  *"the possible roles a singer may play"*

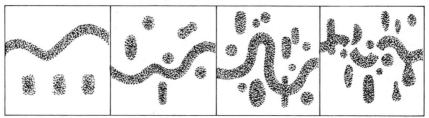

V

| Example | Composer, Title | Date |
|---|---|---|
| 3.14 | Bach, *Suite in B Minor,* overture | c. 1721 |
| 3.15 | Ives, *Three Places in New England,* "Putnam's Camp" | 1903–1914 |

Example 3.14 illustrates the beginning of a *fugue.*

Means and
Possibilities

24

Notice that you hear only one melody line at first, then two, then three, and finally four. The texture becomes increasingly thick and more complex. Notice also that each group of instruments plays the same melody as it enters; that is, the parts enter "in imitation." (See also the imitation in Examples D2.7, D2.8, and D2.9.)

Example 3.15 effectively illustrates how sound relationships contribute to the total effect of a piece. Notice the variety created by: few to many instruments, a wide range of tone colors (produced by different kinds of instruments), and striking contrasts in the relationships among the parts.

**Exercise 1**
**Sound and Texture**
**(side 3)**

The primary purpose of the exercises in this book is to provide you with some additional experience in listening within a particular framework. Their secondary purpose is to present self-correcting material through which you can discover how well you have learned to make discriminations within this framework. The exercises are a "test" only in this sense.

At the beginning of each exercise you will find a

Sound
Relationships

description of the problem and blanks for answering the questions. In the chart following the examples (on a separate page) you will find the correct answers. We suggest the following procedure for each exercise:

1. Study the problem and the specific questions.
2. Do the first three questions and check the answers against the answer chart to see if you are doing better than guessing. If not, go back and do the three questions again.
3. Finish the exercise and check your answers. You may want to listen to the whole exercise again while checking. This procedure will give you a chance not only to correct yourself but to hear again a "demonstration" within the framework of the particular problem described.

Exercise 1 is a further exploration of various kinds of sound relationships. In Examples 1.1–1.9 the instruments or voices play different roles in relation to one another. Match each excerpt with the correct statement below.

A.  One instrument (or voice) plays a *dominant* role

| Example | A | B | C |
|---------|---|---|---|
| 1.1     |   |   |   |
| 1.2     |   |   |   |
| 1.3     |   |   |   |
| 1.4     |   |   |   |
| 1.5     |   |   |   |
| 1.6     |   |   |   |
| 1.7     |   |   |   |
| 1.8     |   |   |   |
| 1.9     |   |   |   |

Means and
Possibilities

while the other instruments play a clearly subordinate accompaniment.

B. The melody is the upper "layer" of a series of chords—all of the parts move along together and thus the accompaniment has no distinguishable character of its own.

C. The instruments (voices) move independently of one another; all are of relatively *equal* importance.

Examples 1.10–1.13 illustrate changes in textural density within an excerpt as well as unchanging textural density. Match each excerpt with the correct statement below.

A. The number of instruments increases.
B. The number of instruments decreases.
C. The number of instruments remains the same.

| Example | A | B | C |
|---|---|---|---|
| 1.10 | | | |
| 1.11 | | | |
| 1.12 | | | |
| 1.13 | | | |

Notice in listening to these examples the dramatic effect that a sudden change in the number of instruments creates. Notice, too, how your first contact with a given excerpt often sets up assumptions as to the sound world of the piece with which the composer can then play.

In Examples 1.14–1.21 the relationship among the strands of texture (the relative dominance of one or their relative equality) changes within the course of the excerpt, or in some examples remains the same. Thus, with striking effect, we experience a change from one kind of texture to another. Match each excerpt with the correct statement.

Sound
Relationships

27

A. One dominant part changes to several parts sharing or vying for the foreground role.
B. Several parts sharing or vying for the foreground role change to one dominant part.
C. There is no change in the relationship among the parts.

| Example | | A | B | C |
|---|---|---|---|---|
| 1.14 | | | | |
| 1.15 | | | | |
| 1.16 | | | | |
| 1.17 | | | | |
| 1.18 | | | | |
| 1.19 | | | | |
| 1.20 | | | | |
| 1.21 | | | | |

Correct
Answers

| Example | Composer, Title | A | B | C |
|---|---|---|---|---|
| 1.1 | Verdi, *La Traviata*, aria (D3.10), 1853 | X | | |
| 1.2 | Bach, *St. Matthew Passion* (D3.5), 1729 | | X | |
| 1.3 | *Desconforté ai esté / Amas qui m'a* (motet) (D3.8), 13th century | | | X |
| 1.4 | Beethoven, *Symphony 7*, 1811–1812 | | X | |
| 1.5 | Mozart, *Horn Concerto 2*, 1783 | X | | |
| 1.6 | Ward, *Upon a Bank with Roses*, 1613 | | | X |
| 1.7 | Hindemith, *Mathis der Maler*, 1934 | | X | |
| 1.8 | Bach, *Suite in B Minor*, c. 1721 | X | | |
| 1.9 | Beethoven, *Quartet*, Opus 59, no. 3, 1806 | | | X |

Means and
Possibilities

| Example | Composer, Title | A | B | C |
|---------|-----------------|---|---|---|
| 1.10 | Beethoven, *Symphony 3*, 1803 | | X | |
| 1.11 | Bach, *Brandenburg Concerto 5*, c. 1721 | X | | |
| 1.12 | Bach, *Suite in B Minor*, c. 1721 | | | X |
| 1.13 | Stravinsky, *Firebird Suite*, 1910 | X | | |
| 1.14 | Mozart, *Quartet in G*, 1782 | | X | |
| 1.15 | Bach, *St. John Passion*, recitative and chorus, c. 1723 | X | | |
| 1.16 | Beethoven, *Symphony 3*,[a] 1803 | X | | |
| 1.17 | Palestrina, *Missa In festis Apostolorum*, Agnus Dei, c. 1580 | | | X |
| 1.18 | Mozart, *Symphony 40*, 1788 | | X | |
| 1.19 | Bach, *Cantata 31*,[b] c. 1715 | X | | |
| 1.20 | Debussy, *Prélude à l'Après-midi d'un Faune*, 1894 | | | X |
| 1.21 | Beethoven, *Symphony 3*,[c] 1803 | | X | |

[a] Note that in this example there are three phases of textural change. The piece progresses from the first, in which there is one dominant part, through an intermediary phase, to a third phase, in which the texture is characterized by great activity in the competition among the parts.

[b] This piece begins with only one melody line which is played in unison by all the instruments of the group.

[c] This excerpt has been included because it is such an extraordinary example of the dramatic effect of textural change. More "lifelike" than some of the earlier examples, it moves through several phases—from an active, complex texture generating tremendous tension, to a gradual lessening of this tension through clarification and simplification of the texture.

## ADDITIONAL
## MATERIALS

The examples suggested here[2] illustrate an additional aspect of sound relationships not included in the previous demonstrations as well as some works in which sound plays a crucial role in the *organization* of the music.

I

Haydn, *Symphony 8,* first movement, c. 1761
Debussy, *La Mer,* 1903–1905
Lully, *Armide,* overture, 1686
Gibbons, *Fantasia a 4,* c. 1608
Mahler, *Symphony 1,* first movement, 1888

The first group of examples illustrates differences in the immediate, purely sensuous aspect of music. Listen to the Haydn symphony and Debussy's *La Mer,* noting the striking difference in sound which results from different instrumental combinations and different uses of these combinations. In the Ancillary Reading section under Musical Instruments (see p. 279), notice the difference in the size of two orchestras and the greater variety of instruments used by the later composer. In addition, note that Haydn uses his orchestra in order to reinforce the musical design. Contrasts in instrumentation, for example, tend to coincide with and help to articulate such musical events as the advent of a new theme or the beginning of a new phrase or section. Debussy, on the other hand, uses his orchestra as an end in itself. In his sensuous *La Mer,* we hear how contrasting instrumental colors, contrasts in density of texture, and

[2] Pieces discussed in Additional Materials are for outside listening and are not included in the accompanying recordings.

the extramusical associations of particular qualities of sound generate the events of the piece. (Which of these works would lose the most if transcribed for the piano?)

The Lully and Gibbons pieces are both written for a group of strings, but Lully's orchestra is large, suited for a public performance, while the Gibbons piece, scored for only four solo viols, sounds small and intimate. (Note that the recordings may distort this kind of difference since the decibel level tends to be equalized for all records by the sound engineers. Thus, the enormous difference in a live performance by 50 musicians and one by 4 musicians is often lost on a recording. This among other factors should encourage you to "Support live music.") The Mahler example is chosen to demonstrate another large and varied orchestra used in a way quite different from Debussy's, although the actual instruments present on the stage are nearly the same as are used in *La Mer*. In what ways is Mahler's use of the orchestra unlike Debussy's; in what ways is it similar to Haydn's?


II

Stravinsky, *Firebird Suite,* finale, 1910
Moussorgsky, *Khovantchina,* prelude, 1873–1881
Stravinsky, *Le Sacre du printemps,* Rondes printanières, 1913
Beethoven, *Symphony 3,* finale, 1803
Beethoven, *Trio,* Opus 11, theme and variations, 1798


This group of pieces illustrates the composer's use of texture and sonority as a basis for organization, that is, to create motion or contrast and to articulate sections.

In the finale of the *Firebird Suite* note how Stravinsky repeats the melody a number of times, hanging different colors on this melodic constant at each of its repetitions. The effect is cumulative and climactic. We move from the opening solo horn statement to the *fortissimo* full orchestra at the conclusion. The Moussorgsky piece has a point of similarity with the *Firebird,* namely, that the composer maneuvers the orchestra in relation to a melodic constant. The excerpt from *Le Sacre du printemps* is more complex: listen carefully, noting the changes that occur in (1) timbre, (2) range of instruments (high and low), (3) activity and density of texture, and (4) foreground-background relationships. These changes contribute significantly to the articulation of the four basic sections of the excerpt.

The Beethoven symphony movement is radically different from the others, for it has fundamentally different goals. While in the first three examples the course of events is highly dependent on the manipulation of sound (as in Debussy's *La Mer*), manipulation of sound in the Beethoven example tends rather to *reinforce* the course of events (as in Haydn's *Symphony 8*). Some of the dramatic changes in texture and sonority in this movement were illustrated previously in Exercise 1. Listen to these and other striking changes in texture and sonority now within the context of the whole movement.

The final movement of Beethoven's *Trio,* Opus 11, is less immediately striking in its sound contrasts, because the composer uses a smaller and less varied group of instruments. However, close listening will reveal a remarkable variety of sounds within the small ensemble of clarinet, cello, and piano. You will notice that a particular sonority or texture remains constant for relatively long periods, helping to articulate the *larger* divisions of the

Means and
Possibilities

structure. For example, following a section in which all three instruments participate (the theme), there is a section for piano alone (Variation 1), which is followed by a section for cello and clarinet alone (Variation 2; see D2.8). Notice that there is also a change in the activity of the texture from the theme to Variation 2: the single line with accompaniment of the theme changes to two equal parts played in imitation in Variation 2. In Variation 3 the piano functions as an accompaniment, first to the clarinet and then to the cello; while in Variation 4 the piano sound alternates with the clarinet-cello sound. Listen to the whole movement, noting as carefully as possible the characteristics of each change in texture and sonority. (Then listen to it again just for the pure pleasure of savoring the marvelous play of sounds.)

Sound
Relationships

Woman Playing a Viol
Tobias Stimmer, c. 1540
(Prints Division, The New York Public Library)

# TIME AND MOVEMENT 3

Demonstration 4

Fundamentals
of
Rhythm
(side 4)

This demonstration provides you with examples and some discussion of the most basic means of organizing time in music. Unlike the previous demonstrations, this demonstration presents much of the discussion on the record itself. For your convenience, certain fundamental concepts which are illustrated on the record are also noted and defined below in the order in which they occur on the record. Read over this material first and refer to it again as the recorded discussion proceeds. A series of practice problems is also included.

*Beat.* That which marks off the passing of time into regular units.

*Meter.* The organization of the pulse or beat into groups which mark off longer but equally regular units of time. When the groups have two beats, the meter is duple; when the groups have three beats, the meter is triple.

Practice Problems

These examples are to be used for practice in determining the meter of a piece. However, this activity should in no sense be considered a primary goal in listening to music. We are simply asking you to make conscious what is fundamentally an immediate physical phenomenon, so that it may serve as a basis from which to work. If you have any difficulty in determining the meter of a piece, you may try the following:

1. Clap the regular beat.
2. Clap only the accented beat.
3. Clap all the beats, calling the accented beat "one." See how far you can count before you must say "one" again.
4. If you can count to two or a multiple of two, the meter is duple. If you can count to three, the meter is triple.

**DUPLE METER**  **TRIPLE METER**

Listen to Examples 4.1 to 4.7 and decide whether they are in duple or in triple meter. After each example you will be given the correct answer.

| Example | Composer, Title | Duple | Triple |
|---------|-----------------|-------|--------|
| 4.1 | Rossini, *William Tell*, overture, 1829 | | |
| 4.2 | J. Strauss, *Emperor Waltz*, 1888 | | |
| 4.3 | Mozart, *Eine kleine Nachtmusik*, 1787 | | |
| 4.4 | Haydn, *Symphony 88*, 1787 | | |

Means and
Possibilities

| 4.5 | Bach, *Brandenburg Concerto 5,* c. 1721 | | |
| 4.6 | Bizet, *Carmen,* 1875 | | |
| 4.7 | Beethoven, *Quartet,* Opus 18, no. 1, 1799 | | |

*Durational relationships.* The relative length of successive tones.

*Tempo.* The rate of speed of the underlying pulse.

Duration and tempo are obviously interrelated and can be measured with a timepiece. The device that is used is called a *metronome.* Through an adjustable pendulum, the metronome makes it possible to indicate tempo—the precise number of beats per minute. For example, an undifferentiated drum beat could be indicated thus, ♩ ♩ ♩ ♩ ♩, with a metronomic indication of ♩ = 120. This means that there would be 120 drum beats per minute, or two drum beats per second.

Duration is notated in music by symbols which relate to one another by a multiple of two—that is, notes which are either twice as long as the next shortest or half the length of the next longest. See Example 1 and the Ancillary Reading, p. 294.

**Example 1** 𝅝 = ♩ ♩

♩ = ♩ ♩

♩ = ♪ ♪ or ♫

♪ = ♪ ♪ or ♫

Knowing this notation and having determined the tempo as, for instance, ♩ = 120, the performer is prepared to play all indicated durations.

The following rhythmic configurations each "oc-

Time and
Movement

cupy" the same amount of time and would equal one metric unit in triple meter (or one and one-half seconds at $\quarternote = 120$—a totally nonfunctional and nonmusical piece of information):

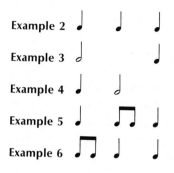

Establish a pulse and clap Examples 2 through 6.

Notice that while pulse and meter are both regular, rhythmic configurations can be irregular. However, they are perceived within the framework of beat and meter. Clap example 7 and tap the pulse with your foot.[1]

You can easily recognize the relationship between the varying, that is, irregular, durations of the rhythmic pattern, and the regular durations of the underlying pulse.

Now try Example 8. A rhythmic pattern is presented by the Violin I here. It is combined with two other layers of "rhythm" below. With two other students, clap the example.

[1]Bar lines mark off the regular grouping of the beats, and — equals a strong, accented beat, ⌣ a weak, unaccented beat.

**Example 8**[2]

VIOLIN I

VIOLIN II

BASS

*Downbeat.* The accented beat, that is, the first beat
of each metric unit.

*Upbeat.* The unaccented beat preceding the downbeat, that is, the last notes of each metric group. This
terminology reflects the conductor's upward motion
(and its concomitant tension) on the "upbeat" and
his downward motion (and the concomitant release
of tension) on the accented or "downbeat."

*Compound meter.* A combination of duple and triple
meter. In compound duple meter, each beat is subdivided into three to form six beats (two groups of
three beats each); while in ordinary duple meter each
beat is subdivided into two to form four beats (two
groups of two beats each). Compound duple meter,
especially in a slow tempo, may be perceived as triple
meter, where each group of three is heard as a metric
unit in itself.

If Examples 9 and 10 are played one after the other,

**Example 9**   Duple meter

**Example 10**   Compound duple meter

[2]A dot after a note is equal to one-half the durational value
of that note; for example, a dotted eighth note ($\flat$), as in this
example, is equal to an eighth note plus a sixteenth note ($\flat\flat$)
(equal to three sixteenths). For further information on rhythmic
notation, see Ancillary Reading.

Time and
Movement

39

keeping the duration of each group of eighth notes the same (that is, maintaining the *beat* at a constant tempo), then the duration of the individual eighth notes will differ.

Establish a pulse with your foot and then clap Example 11.

**Example 11**

Examples 12 and 13 (from Beethoven's *Symphony 9, scherzo*) are illustrated on the record; the tempo is very fast.

**Example 12**

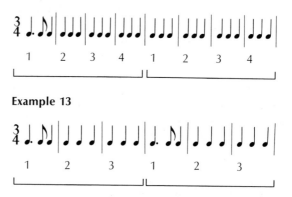

**Example 13**

# Demonstration 5
## The Experience
## of Rhythm
## (side 5)

Be sure to read carefully the comments concerning the examples in this demonstration. You will probably find it most useful first to read the comments for each example or group of examples, then to listen to the example, and then stop to read the comments for the next example. You may need to go back and listen to some of the examples more than once. Do not simply listen to the record straight through.

In the previous demonstration fundamentals of rhythmic organization were illustrated and discussed. In this demonstration we are concerned with ways in which rhythmic factors can be used to create different effects in music.

I

| Example | Composer, Title | Date |
|---------|-----------------|------|
| 5.1 | Haydn, *Symphony 88,* minuet | 1787 |
| 5.2 | Ravel, *Daphnis et Chloé* | 1909–1912 |
| 5.3 | Rossini, *William Tell,* overture, opening | 1829 |
| 5.4 | Rossini, *William Tell,* overture, later | 1829 |

**5.1** *"a pulse is clearly audible"*          **5.2** *"no distinguishable pulse"*

Time and
Movement

The first group of examples has been chosen to demonstrate the fundamental, almost physical, role of the pulse in creating different musical effects. The first nine examples demonstrate the differences in effect between pieces in which a pulse is clearly audible (Example 5.1) and those in which it is not (Example 5.2). Examples 5.3 and 5.4 illustrate this same contrast within a single piece.

| Example | Composer, Title | Date |
|---------|-----------------|------|
| 5.5 | *Saeta* (Flamenco) | |
| 5.6 | *Veni Creator Spiritus* (Gregorian Chant) | |
| 5.7 | *Maru-Bihag* (Indian) | |
| 5.8 | Stravinsky, *Le Sacre du printemps,* beginning | 1913 |
| 5.9 | Stravinsky, *Le Sacre du printemps,* Danse sacrale | 1913 |

Examples 5.5 and 5.6 are both unaccompanied chants. Example 5.5 has no distinguishable pulse, while in Example 5.6 notes (or syllables) of equal duration tend to create a regular pulse. (What is the function of the notes of longer duration?) Example 5.7 differs from 5.5 and 5.6 in that the *accompaniment* creates a regular and strong pulse.

Compare Examples 5.8 and 5.9 considering the absence or presence of a pulse and the resulting differences in effect.

II

Examples 5.10 and 5.11 both have a clear, strong pulse. In what way are the beats grouped differently?

It is obvious that in Example 5.11 the beats are clearly organized in pairs, in a regular pattern of

| Example | Composer, Title | Date |
|---------|-----------------|------|
| 5.10 | Stravinsky, *Octet for Wind Instruments* | 1923–1924 |
| 5.11 | Sousa, *Stars and Stripes Forever* | 1896 |

alternation of strong and weak beats—that is, *duple meter*. In Example 5.10, on the other hand, there are many moments in which we hear a regularly recurring accent; yet no sooner do we begin to settle into this duple pattern than the composer expands or contracts a measure (the group of two beats), shifting the accent, changing the meter, and in this fashion keeping us always off balance.

Listen again to the four examples listed below (chosen from Part I), for they further illustrate the difference in effect between pieces which have a clear pulse with a clear meter, and those which have a clear pulse but (at best) ambiguous meter.

Example 5.1. This piece is in triple meter.

Example 5.7. Meter, if it functions at all in this piece, marks off very large time units. (You may be aware of the duple division of the beat, but it is extremely difficult to discover the pattern of grouping of the slower beats.)

Example 5.4. This is an example of duple meter.

Example 5.9. While there is an extremely powerful pulse, the meter is ambiguous and plays a subordinate role.

| Example | Composer, Title | Date |
|---------|-----------------|------|
| 5.12 | Tchaikovsky, *Symphony 6*, second movement | 1893 |

Example 5.12 is regular in its organization of the pulse, but the grouping is unusual. The meter is quintuple, but the groups of five can be divided

into two plus three. Thus one can count 1-2-3-4-5
or 1-2, 1-2-3.

III

| Example | Composer, Title | Date |
| --- | --- | --- |
| 5.13 | Tchaikovsky, *Marche slave* | 1876 |
| 5.14 | M. Dixon and R. Henderson, *Bye Bye Blackbird* (performed by Miles Davis Quintet, 1956) | 1926 |
| 5.15 | Schubert, *Quintet in C,* Opus 163, scherzo | 1828 |
| 5.16 | Beethoven, *Symphony 3,* first movement | 1803 |
| 5.17 | Tchaikovsky, *Francesca da Rimini* | 1877 |

Examples 5.13–5.17 demonstrate some possibilities
for creating rhythmic conflict against either the
beat or the meter. This effect is called *syncopation.*
In Example 5.13, for instance, notice that the melody creates a clear duple meter with accents on

**5.13** *"syncopation"*

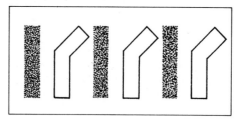

the first and third beats of a four-beat group. But
on the "off" or weak beats (two and four) the rest
of the orchestra creates an accent which conflicts
with the metrical accents of the melody. Notice
how, when the conflicting accents stop, the tension lessens.

Jazz is almost always described in terms of synco-

Means and
Possibilities

pation. In Example 5.14, a jazz piece, we hear, as the foundation, drums and double bass setting forth a metronomic, four-beat (duple) meter. In conflict with this basic pulse, the piano plays chords (the harmonic foundation), many of which do not coincide with the beats. Finally, the muted trumpet plays its free, highly syncopated version of a familiar tune.

Example 5.15 begins with a clear, regularly accented pulse. As was pointed out in Demonstration 4, tempo can influence your perception of meter. Thus, in this piece the beats are grouped regularly in threes (triple meter), but because of the quick tempo, you are more likely to hear a slower pulse made up of the first beat of each of these groups of three. This pulse is generally grouped in fours. Tension increases when the upper strings set up an accent against the basic pulse by consistently *anticipating* the downbeat. Tension is relaxed when all the strings come back together on the beat.

Example 5.16 includes (in this order): (1) a shift of accent—the accent is shifted to the second beat in the basic triple meter, (2) a momentary shift into duple meter, (3) a loss of the downbeat altogether (silence on the downbeat), and (4) once more a momentary shift into duple meter. Notice, again, the tension and instability created when the meter is disrupted, and the relaxation of tension and return to stability as the meter becomes clear.

**5.16** *"the tension and instability created when the meter is disrupted"*

Example 5.17 illustrates another kind of rhythmic conflict—two meters superimposed on each other. In this piece, the melody is generally in triple meter, and the accompaniment is in compound duple meter.[3]

IV

| Example | Composer, Title | Date |
|---------|-----------------|------|
| 5.18 | Berlioz, *Symphonie fantastique,* first movement | 1830 |
| 5.19 | Bartok, *Sonata for Two Pianos and Percussion* | 1937 |
| 5.20 | Berg, *Lyric Suite* | 1925–1926 |
| 5.21 | Beethoven, *Symphony 3,* fourth movement | 1803 |
| 5.22 | Mozart, *Quartet in G,* K. 387, fourth movement | 1782 |
| 5.23 | Bach, *Cantata 31* | c. 1715 |
| 5.24 | Mahler, *Symphony 1* | 1888 |
| 5.25 | Beethoven: *String Quartet,* Opus 18, no. 1 | 1799 |

Examples 5.18–5.25 demonstrate changes in the rate at which the pulse is moving (changes in tempo) and changes in rhythmic activity without a change in tempo (more or fewer notes per beat). In Example 5.18 the pulse becomes slower; this is called a *ritardando.* In Example 5.19 the pulse becomes faster—an *accelerando.* Example 5.20 includes first an *accelerando* and then a *ritardando.*

Examples 5.21 and 5.22 show an increase in rhyth-

[3]Notice that this metric conflict creates a kind of textural activity different from that of earlier examples. In the examples in Demonstration 3, activity is the result of rhythmic and melodic independence of the parts which vie for the foreground role; whereas in this piece it is the *metrical* conflict between foreground (melody) and background (accompaniment) which is the source of the textural activity.

Means and
Possibilities

mic activity with no change in tempo. The second segment of Example 5.21 is a varied repetition of the first; the melody remains the same in both segments, but in the second, the surrounding parts have three notes per beat rather than two. Example 5.22 begins with notes of long duration—slow rhythmic motion—and changes to much faster rhythmic motion. The tempo, however, remains essentially the same throughout. Notice that, paradoxically, while there is little rhythmic activity in the first section, it is active in texture; in the second section, where the rhythm becomes more active, the texture is less active—that is, there is one clear melodic line with simple accompaniment. In Example 5.23, on the other hand, there is an increase

**5.23** *"an increase in both rhythmic and textural activity"*

in both rhythmic and textural activity, although the faster rhythmic motion anticipates the increase in textural activity.

Examples 5.24 and 5.25 illustrate a decrease in rhythmic activity over a steady pulse (with no change in tempo). Example 5.24 demonstrates what is called a "written-out *ritardando*"; while a steady pulse is maintained in the lower part of the texture, the tones in the rest of the texture gradually become further and further apart in time. In Example 5.25 we hear a striking change from relatively rapid to slower rhythmic motion (fewer notes per beat). The passage is a preparation for and return to the main theme of the movement. Notice that it is with

Time and
Movement

the entrance of the melody that the rhythmic
motion slows down, and that the texture also
becomes much less active.

Means and
Possibilities

## ADDITIONAL MATERIALS

Demonstrations 4 and 5 focused your listening on specific and rather isolated aspects of rhythmic organization and their varying effects. We suggest, now, a more active participation in the musical process, which should contribute to more responsive listening: several students together might constitute themselves a "rhythm band," either with toy or actual percussion instruments or simply with clapping or rapping. One player can establish the pulse, another the meter by "playing" only the downbeats, then one or two others can beat various patterns, introducing syncopation or even changes of meter. Three possible rhythmic combinations are given as examples.

I

**Example 1**

**Example 2**

**Example 3**

II

Rossini, *William Tell,* overture, 1829
Mozart, *Don Giovanni,* "La ci darem la mano" (duet), 1787
Moussorgsky, *Khovantchina,* prelude, 1873–1881

Listen first to the main part of the *William Tell* overture (after the slow introduction). Discover and clap, at a slower tempo if necessary, its predominant rhythmic pattern (which lent itself so well to accompanying a certain famous horseback rider). See if you can notate it. Then listen for other layers of rhythmic activity in the piece and clap them. Several students can do this together. How many patterns can you find occurring simultaneously? Can you tap two of them at a time, one with each hand? When and how is the predominant rhythmic pattern abandoned? What is the difference in effect as the rhythmic organization changes? (These are questions that you might ask of any piece you listen to.)

Next, listen to the Mozart duet and Moussorgsky's prelude to *Khovantchina*. After noting the beat and the grouping of the beats (meter) in each piece, try to find the still larger rhythmic divisions of the structure—the length of musical impulses or phrases. Move with the music (using your arm or walking) from one goal, or point of rest, to the next, trying to sense the relative time intervals. You will

Means and
Possibilities

50

be responding to the structural rhythm, or phrase rhythm, of the piece. You will probably observe that the Mozart is regular or symmetrical in phrase rhythm—that all the phrases are of equal length—while Moussorgsky's work is less predictable due to its irregular or asymmetrical phrase rhythm. (You can determine this more precisely by counting the number of measures from one point of rest to the next. In the duple meter of the Mozart duet, you will find that there are an equal number of down-beats, and thus measures, in each phrase, while in the Moussorgsky piece the number of downbeats varies from one phrase to the next.) The question of phrase rhythm is discussed further in Demonstration 6.

III

Vivaldi, *Concerto*, Opus 3, no. 3, first movement, c. 1712
Bach, *Brandenburg Concerto 2*, first movement, c. 1721
Bach, *St. Matthew Passion*, "Blute nur" (aria), 1729

Listen carefully to the works listed above. In these pieces note that one does not have the same sense of motion directed toward frequently occurring, clear goals where the motion seems temporarily to stop; but rather a more continuous sense of motion which actually stops only at widely spaced time intervals. See if you can determine what, other than the pulse, articulates the rhythmic structure between these widely spaced goals—what are the rhythmic stepping stones? (For further discussion of this subject, see Demonstration 6, particularly the discussion of *sequence.*)

In discussing structural rhythm we have passed into an area in which melodic and rhythmic factors can no longer be separated, since, in fact, structural rhythm is a function of melodic shape as well as

Time and
Movement

51

a number of other factors—harmony, for example. We introduce it here to give you a first awareness of rhythm in its largest sense, namely, the way a piece as a whole moves as a result of all its combined attributes.[4]

[4]In considering any whole piece, a discussion of rhythm might take into account (going from shorter to longer durational units) beat, meter, rhythmic patterns, sequence, phrase, groups of phrases, and sections. Thus, as we can hear upbeats and downbeats, we can, by analogy, hear upbeat phrases and downbeat phrases, preparation passages and arrival passages, stable sections and unstable sections. This kind of involvement, along with the immediate sensuous aspect, provides the most directly physical avenue to the musical experience.

Means and
Possibilities

*Lady with a Lute*
Johannes Vermeer (1632–1675)
(The Metropolitan Museum of Art, New York;
bequest of Collis P. Huntington, 1925)

# PITCH AND MOVEMENT  *4*

The most general aspect of *pitch* in music is described, perhaps unfortunately, in the spatial terms "high" and "low." We speak of pitch moving "higher" or "lower," or "up" or "down." The difference between high and low is also described with the term "register"; thus, the same tune can be played in a high register (on the flute) or in a low register (on the bassoon), or it may be sung by men or by women. Except for the register, the tune will sound the same; that is, the two instruments (or voices) will play the same notes separated by one or more octaves.

In order to understand the phenomenon of the *octave*, we must consider the individual pitches which form the fundamental sound material of music. Music is not generally made up of a continuum of sounds moving up or down. (Such a continuum, like the sound produced by a siren, can be created by the human voice and by certain instruments, such as the violin and cello, when the player slides his finger up or down the string while bowing.) In music, a selection has been made from this continuum which results in a series or ladder of discrete pitches. Moving upward from any one pitch, and playing all the tones in order, we find that after 12 different pitches have been played (the *chromatic scale*), the pitches are repeated in a higher register. This repetition of the pitches in different registers exemplifies the phenomenon of the octave.

Putting it another way, this particular selection of 12 pitches from the pitch continuum divides the octave into 12 equidistant tones. These tones constitute all the different pitches generally found in Western music; they are separated from one another by a *half step*. An *interval* is the distance between any two tones; the half step is the smallest interval. (See the Ancillary Reading section for further discussion of intervals.) The next largest interval is the whole step. The octave can be divided into *six* equidistant pitches separated by whole steps. (This is the whole-tone scale—note the striking difference in effect between this scale and the chromatic scale.)

The octave can also be divided into seven different pitches separated by a series of whole and half steps creating a number of different *modes*. Two of these, the major and minor modes, provide the fundamental pitch material for Western music from the seventeenth to the twentieth century—some composers still think in terms of them.[1] It should be emphasized that the notion of a scale or mode is an abstraction derived from the actual pitch material of melodies. Instead of presenting the major scale, then, as an entity, we will demonstrate how it can be derived from a familiar melody, *America*. (For information on pitch notation see the Ancillary Reading, p. 297.)

If we now order the pitches which occur in this

[1]Before the seventeenth century other modes were described by theorists and given names derived from ancient Greek music, for example, Dorian, Phrygian, and Lydian.

Means and
Possibilities

**Example 1**

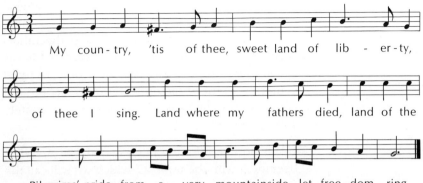

My coun-try, 'tis of thee, sweet land of lib - er-ty,

of thee I sing. Land where my fathers died, land of the

Pil-grims' pride, from e - very mountainside let free-dom ring.

piece from the lowest to the highest, the result is
as shown in Example 2.

**Example 2**

This, then, is the pitch material of the melody. Now
sing the tune and determine which pitch sounds
the most stable, the most at rest; then sing or play
the pitches as ordered in Example 2, again determining which is the most stable. In both cases you
probably found that the note G, the tone with
which the melody both begins and ends, sounds
most final. Indeed, the sense of completeness, of
finality, at the end of *America* is generated to a
large extent by the function which the note G has
acquired through its contact with the specific collection of pitches in this melody. The point must
be emphasized that the stability or instability—that
is, the function—of a particular pitch derives from
its relation to the other pitches which surround it.
Within a different collection of pitches this same
note might sound very unstable; the function or
"meaning" of a pitch, then, is always *relative* (see

Pitch and
Movement

Demonstration 8). In a given context of pitches, the one that sounds most stable has a special position—it becomes the central tone in relation to which we hear all the others, and the others seem to gravitate toward it.[2] This central tone is called the *tonic.* The existence of a tonic, or tonal center, is a crucial factor in the organization and comprehensibility of music between approximately 1650 and 1900.

Let us now reorder the pitch material of *America,* beginning with the tonic, *G,* which we will call the *first degree* in recognition of its central position.

**Example 3**

We have now derived the G Major scale. Using it as a model we can discover exactly what combina-

[2]Music theorists have discussed at length the question of whether this phenomenon is inherent in the natural properties of sound or whether it is the result of musical conditioning.

Means and
Possibilities

tion of whole and half steps generates the major mode and can then build a major scale starting on any pitch. The simplest way to *see* the whole step–half step arrangement is by looking at the piano keyboard (although the best way would be to *hear* the difference between whole and half steps). Looking at the diagram of the piano keyboard, you can observe the following: The distance between any two adjacent keys (including black keys) is a half step; thus, G to A is a whole step, since there is a black key between, but B to C is a half step since there is no black key between. So the G Major scale has the following arrangement of whole and half steps:

| DEGREE: | 1 | 2 | 3 | 4 | 5 | 6 | 7 | 8 |
|---------|---|---|---|---|---|---|---|---|
| PITCH: | G | A | B | C | D | E | F♯ | G |
| INTERVAL: | 1 | 1 | ½ | 1 | 1 | 1 | ½ | |

An important characteristic of this model is its division into two symmetrical parts: Degrees 1–4 and Degrees 5–8, the two parts being separated by a whole step. Using this model, then, we can build a major scale starting on, for example, F (Example 4).

**Example 4**

Try building scales starting on other pitches using the model and the piano keyboard.

A model for the minor scale (Example 5) is only

useful through the first five degrees, since the upper part may take several different forms (see the Ancillary Reading, p. 300.)

**Example 5**

Notice that the distinguishing difference in the minor mode lies in the half step between the second and third degrees as compared to the whole step that exists in the major mode.

In the light of our discussion of the major scale, turn back now to *America.* You will hear that the melody is organized in two parts, the first ending with "of thee I sing." This first part is organized around the tonic note—it begins there, moves below, above, and through it, and finally returns to it. The second part of the melody moves to the fifth degree of the scale and minimizes the first degree until it returns to it at the end. This organization of the melody reflects somewhat the organization of the scale into two halves, and points up the significance of the fifth degree (the starting point of the second half) as the second "pillar" of the tonal structure. The fifth degree is called (misleadingly) the *dominant.* Its significance is further discussed in Demonstration 8.

You may further observe that this melody is very *conjunct*—that is, it avoids leaps or large intervals (making it easy to sing). The most noticeable leap occurs between the two halves of the melody, the leap of a fifth from the tonic to the dominant. Notice, too, that it is confined within a range of

Means and
Possibilities

a seventh and that it gradually ascends within this range, then quickly descends through it in the final two measures.

To summarize, then, we have moved from the most general aspects of pitch—high and low—to a selection from this continuum—the 12 pitches forming the entire pitch material of Western music—to a further selection—the seven different pitches of the major and minor modes which can be built from specific arrangements of whole and half steps. The most significant aspect of this selection is its creation of a hierarchy of stability–instability among the resulting pitches.

Having considered to some extent the pitch relationships in *America*, let us consider, now, how the melody moves through time, that is, the rhythmic patterns out of which the melody is made and which contribute to its unity and variety. Tap the rhythm of the melody. Note that there is a rhythmic pattern (*motive*) repeated, with slight variations, a number of times: ♩ ♩ ♩ | ♩. ♪♩ |. This underlying figure helps to unify the melody. Note that in the third statement ("of thee I sing") the last two notes are dropped and the fourth note is extended: ♩ ♩ ♩ | ♩.. The rhythmic activity of the phrase, not its length, is lessened as it comes to rest on the longer note. This dotted half note is also the tonic and marks off a section of the song both rhythmically and tonally. The second and concluding section contains four statements of the pattern. The first two are rhythmically identical[3] with the first two statements of the song. These are followed by two statements which give variety to the song by manipulating the basic pattern and at the same

[3]They are also the same in melodic shape—the second statement begins one scale degree lower than the first (a *sequence*).

time reach a climax both in pitch and rhythmic activity. The first: ♩ ♫ ♫ | ♩. ♪♪ | is followed by: ♫ ♩ ♩ | ♩. |

# Demonstration 6

## Melodic Motion
### and Shape
### (side 6)

We turn now from the basic attributes of pitch and the fundamentals of pitch organization, as illustrated in a simple melody, to more complex melodies and some of the factors which determine their character.

| Example | Composer, Title | Date |
|---------|-----------------|------|
| 6.1 | Mozart, *Sonata in A*, K. 331 | 1778 |

Listen to Example 6.1 which is notated as shown.

**Example 6.1**

Remembering our consideration of rhythmic motives in *America*, you will hear that the theme from this Mozart sonata movement also has an underlying rhythmic pattern (motive) which constitutes its fundamental building block and is manipulated in various ways. Clap the rhythm of the opening measure, which provides the rhythmic material for the entire tune:

The second measure repeats the rhythmic and

melodic pattern one step down on the scale, a *sequence.* Next, the second half of the original rhythmic pattern ♩♪ is separated from the first half and stated by itself, then repeated three times (altered the second time so that the last two statements seem to merge). These iterations of the second half of the rhythmic motive move in pitch back up the scale, ending the first phrase inconclusively on the second degree of the A Major scale, and on a weak beat in the $\frac{6}{8}$ meter. The second, and complementary, phrase is almost identical rhythmically, but moves more quickly upward in Measure 7 and then back down, ending much more conclusively on the tonic, with the note of longest duration, and on a metrically strong beat.

A phrase ending is called a *cadence* (from It. *cadere,* "to fall"); the first phrase, then, ends not on the tonic and with a "feminine" cadence—that is, one on a weak beat—the second phrase ends on the tonic and with a "masculine" cadence—one on a strong beat. The resultant effect is of two complementary phrases, the first ending "up in the air," the second with more finality. This is called an antecedent–consequent phrase relationship. Having analyzed in detail the components of this melody, we can see how rhythmic and melodic elements have interacted to create the whole, the experience of which is more than the sum of its parts.

## II

The rest of Demonstration 6 is concerned with two aspects of melodic organization: (1) the intervallic relationship (distance) between successive tones, and (2) the way in which the melody, almost like a living organism, must breathe. We have already referred to the first topic in the discussion of *America,* in which the motion was described as *con-*

*junct,* that is, composed mainly of a stepwise arrangement of tones. In contrast to this are *disjunct* melodies, in which there are larger intervals between successive tones. Another familiar example of a conjunct melody is *Mary Had a Little Lamb,* while *Rock-a-Bye Baby* is a disjunct melody.

**MARY HAD A LITTLE LAMB**

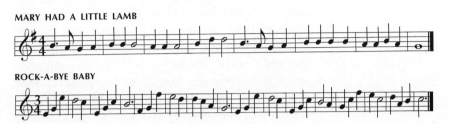

**ROCK-A-BYE BABY**

| Example | Composer, Title | Date |
|---------|-----------------|------|
| 6.2 | Tamil Folk Song (India) | |
| 6.3 | R. Strauss, *Ein Heldenleben* | 1898 |
| 6.4 | Rossini, *The Silken Ladder* (*La Scala di Seta*), overture | 1812 |

Melodies are rarely either conjunct or disjunct *exclusively,* but rather tend more toward one kind of motion or the other. The first two examples in Group II illustrate this difference. In the Indian melody (Example 6.2) only tones adjacent to one another in the exotic scale of this piece are used; in addition, the melody is confined within a small pitch range (the *range* is defined by a melody's

**CONJUNCT MELODY**          **DISJUNCT MELODY**

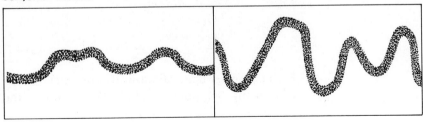

Pitch and
Movement

highest and lowest pitches). In striking contrast, the Strauss melody (Example 6.3) moves predominantly by leaps through a wide range.

In Example 6.4, by Rossini, we find upward leaps at the beginning of each phrase followed by a gradual stepwise descent (a "filling in" of the interval of the leap). Thus, although the melody employs both conjunct and disjunct motion, because of the size and prominence of the leaps and the wide range, the effect is predominantly disjunct. (Note that the tones are played *legato;* that is, they flow smoothly into one another because throughout the melody the soloists play several tones in one breath. This manner of playing, however, is independent of the conjunct or disjunct organization of the melody.)

**Example 6.4**

(first phrase only)

| Example | Composer, Title | Date |
|---------|-----------------|------|
| 6.5 | Beethoven, *Symphony 9,* fourth movement | 1823 |
| 6.6 | Bartok, *Music for Strings, Percussion, and Celesta* | 1936 |
| 6.7 | Berg, *Wozzeck,* death scene | 1915–1917 |
| 6.8 | Vivaldi, *Concerto Grosso,* Opus 3, no. 6, second movement | c. 1712 |

Examples 6.5–6.8 are all basically conjunct. Notice that in the Beethoven melody (Example 6.5) the only significant leaps that occur do so at a crucial

Means and
Possibilities

juncture; namely, at the end of the third phrase and immediately again between that phrase and the next, marking a return to opening material. In an almost exclusively conjunct melody, these two adjacent leaps stand out, helping to articulate the structure (see *America*). This melody also is played *legato*—the cellists do not lift their bows between notes.

Examples 6.6 and 6.7 are both *chromatic* as opposed to *diatonic*—that is, the pitches of the melody are not confined exclusively to a single major or minor scale. The small intervals and limited range of the Bartok melody (Example 6.6) give it a creeping quality, making the few somewhat larger intervals sound much bigger than they actually are (the largest interval is a minor third). In contrast, the excerpt from Berg's *Wozzeck* (Example 6.7) moves *only* in half steps but through a much larger range than the previous example, reflecting effectively the expanding circles of water in which Wozzeck is drowning. Notice also that the "waves" of sound overlap within the texture and begin over and over again. One does not really perceive the intervallic distance between endings and beginnings as leaps, however, but rather simply as a new start. While the solo violin melody in the Vivaldi excerpt (Example 6.8) is fundamentally conjunct, its few leaps stand out and define the units of the melody, as in Example 6.5.

| Example | Composer, Title | Date |
|---------|-----------------|------|
| 6.9 | Haydn, *Sonata for Piano in C* | c. 1794 |
| 6.10 | Mozart, *The Magic Flute*, aria | 1791 |
| 6.11 | Schoenberg, *Herzgewächse* | 1911 |

Examples 6.9–6.11 are basically disjunct. Notice that the Haydn sonata (Example 6.9) is played *staccato*,

especially at the beginning; that is, the tones are detached from one another because the pianist lifts his arm and fingers between one tone and the next. In the Mozart aria (Example 6.10) the large intervals are also sung staccato, but in Schoenberg's piece (Example 6.11) the large intervals are sung legato—the singer "slides" from one tone to the next.

| Example | Composer, Title | Date |
|---------|-----------------|------|
| 6.12 | Mozart, *Symphony 40*, fourth movement | 1788 |
| 6.13 | Stravinsky, *Octet for Wind Instruments*, second movement | 1923–1924 |
| 6.14 | Schubert, *Die Schöne Müllerin*, Ungeduld | 1823 |
| 6.15 | Brahms, *Symphony 3*, first movement | 1883 |

Examples 6.12–6.15 have been chosen to illustrate melodies that include a contrast between conjunct and disjunct motion. The Mozart melody (Example 6.12) demonstrates this contrast in its two brief,

**Example 6.12**

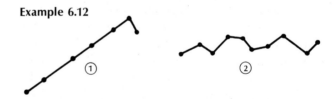

juxtaposed motives—the first disjunct with a relatively large range, the second conjunct with a small range. The melody also contrasts staccato and legato playing. The first, disjunct motive is played staccato; the second, conjunct motive is played more legato. The Stravinsky melody (Example 6.13) is conjunct until the end, when it moves out of its small range with several large leaps.

Perception of a melody as being conjunct or dis-

Means and
Possibilities

junct is influenced by several factors in addition to the actual intervallic distance between its pitches. Among these are the range of the melody together with the effect of its movement as confined or expansive. For example, in the first motive of the Mozart melody (Example 6.12), which we described as being disjunct, the intervals are all fourths and thirds; in the Stravinsky theme (Example 6.13), the first three intervals are also thirds. Yet, the difference between the two examples is striking; there is a sense of "taking off" in Example 6.12 generated by its continuous upward motion through a range of almost two octaves, while in Example 6.13 there is a sense of "turning in," due to the back-and-forth motion within the very small range, delimited by the interval of a third.

In the Schubert song (Example 6.14), there is a contrast between the basically conjunct motion during the first part of the song and the more disjunct motion near the end; this contrast coincides with a change in the text of the song (printed below). Notice that the change to more disjunct

| Ungeduld | Impatience |
|---|---|

| | |
|---|---|
| Ich schnitt' es gern in alle Rinden ein, | I'd carve the words on every tree bark, |
| ich grüb' es gern in jeden Kieselstein, | I'd engrave them on every stone; |
| ich möcht' es sä'n auf jedes frische Beet | I'd write on every garden bed |
| mit Kressensamen, der es schnell verräth | With seeds of cress that swiftly could be read |
| auf jeden weissen Zettel möcht' ich's schreiben: | On every scrap of paper would I write: |
| Dein ist mein Herz, | Yours is my heart, |
| dein ist mein Herz | Yours is my heart |
| und soll es ewig, ewig bleiben. | And it shall be yours forever. |

Pitch and
Movement

motion, together with the rhythmic contrast, markedly alters the character of the music. Two melodies from a single movement are juxtaposed in Example 6.15—the first, disjunct and dramatic; the second, conjunct and lyrical.

III

| Example | Composer, Title | Date |
|---------|-----------------|------|
| 6.16 | Mozart, *Don Giovanni*, duet | 1787 |
| 6.17 | Sousa, *Semper Fidelis* | 1888 |
| 6.18 | Prokofiev, *Classical Symphony*, gavotte | 1916–1917 |
| 6.19 | Milhaud, *La Création du monde* | 1923 |
| 6.20 | *Lamento di Tristano* (medieval dance) | 14th century |

The remaining examples deal with a second aspect of melody—the way in which it breathes. The fact that music "occupies" time is experienced not only on its lower level of temporal organization—pulse, meter, durations, or rhythmic patterns—but also in such larger considerations as the movement of a melody to its goals (see also the earlier discussion in the Additional Materials of Chapter 3). These goals are moments of arrested motion or *caesurae*. The manner in which these goals are reached—the motion of a melody from one goal to another—creates an organic rhythm, crucial to the effect of each piece, which involves the unique relationship of all the dimensions of that piece.

In Examples 6.16–6.20 the melodic units are equal in length; that is, the goals occur at equal time intervals. In other words, in each of these examples a symmetrical rhythmic structure is established by the regular occurrence in time of the moments of arrested motion, or caesurae. (As you listen, try to

discover what elements create these caesurae.) A
clear melodic unit, defined or articulated by its
goal, is called a *phrase;* the symmetrical organization of Examples 6.16–6.20 is described as *balanced
phrase structure.* Notice, however, that the goals
have relative degrees of completeness or finality;
the relationship between and among goals is another crucial aspect of the way in which the listener
follows the music (see Example 6.1 above).

In Example 6.16, also by Mozart, only the last of
the four short phrases reaches a relatively final-

**BALANCED PHRASE STRUCTURE**

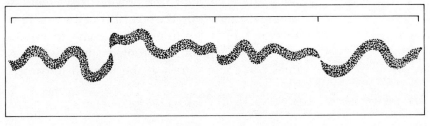

sounding goal. This is, of course, because only the
last phrase ends on the tonic note. Example 6.17
not only illustrates balanced phrase structure but
is also a good example of regular thickening of the
texture; instruments are added with each repetition
of the melody.

In Example 6.19, which has an obvious jazz influence, the chord progression—the harmony of
the accompaniment—is constantly repeated, while
the melody, played by the clarinet, changes freely
with each repetition of the underlying harmony.
(Notice that one of the statements is slightly extended, interrupting the otherwise regular structural rhythm.)

IV

Examples 6.21–6.23 illustrate unbalanced or non-

Pitch and
Movement

| Example | Composer, Title | Date |
|---------|-----------------|------|
| 6.21 | Mozart, *Don Giovanni,* duet | 1787 |
| 6.22 | Schubert, *Die Winterreise,* Frühlingsträume | 1827 |
| 6.23 | Moussorgsky, *Khovantchina,* prelude | 1873–1881 |

symmetrical phrase structure. You will recognize Example 6.21 as Example 6.16 with a continuation. When the soprano takes up the melody, notice that you hear an almost literal repetition until the unexpected extension of the fourth short melodic unit, which interrupts the previously symmetrical phrase rhythm. Thus, the regularity of the structural rhythm, which the listener has come to expect, almost to depend on, is disrupted when the melody does not come to rest at the moment expected.

**6.21** *"the last phrase continues through the moment of anticipated arrival"*

As pointed out above, some phrases end more conclusively than others, and in this fashion a hierarchical relationship among phrases is established. This was illustrated in Example 6.1 and is shown again now in Example 6.21. Here the first two smaller segments taken together constitute the *antecedent phrase,* which ends—inconclusively—on the *dominant.* The next two segments together constitute the *consequent phrase,* which ends—now conclusively—on the *tonic.*

The Schubert song (Example 6.22) is similar to the

Means and
Possibilities

72

**Example 6.21**

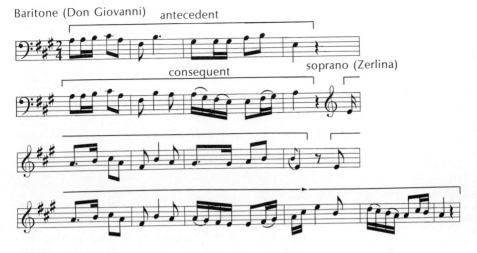

Mozart duet (Example 6.21) in its disruption of the regular structural rhythm: Schubert sets up phrase endings occurring at regular time intervals, but then suddenly in the last phrase continues through the moment of anticipated arrival, extending the phrase and thus upsetting the previously symmetrical structure.

**Example 6.22**

In Example 6.23 by Moussorgsky, however, a normative phrase length is never established—the listener cannot predict when a goal will occur,

**6.23** *"a normative phrase length is never established".*

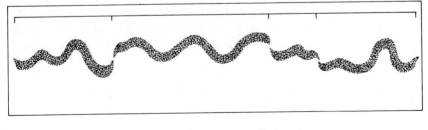

when the melodic motion will come to rest. The effect of this melody, particularly of its sense of freedom, is quite different from that of melodies which have a regular structural rhythm.

V

| Example | Composer, Title | Date |
|---------|-----------------|------|
| 6.24 | *Salve Regina* (Gregorian Chant) | Middle Ages |

While Examples 6.21–6.23 differed from Examples 6.16–6.20 in regularity of structural rhythm, all these examples are fundamentally similar in that the melodic unit is clearly articulated. Their melodic motion is characterized by a succession of delimited melodic units, and the listener follows the melody through each phrase from one goal to the next, comparing the goals as they appear. Example 6.24 is introduced as a link between this kind of melodic organization and that found in the concluding examples. In this Gregorian Chant (Example 6.24) one certainly hears melodic motion delimited by caesurae—the melody stops, the singers breathe. The listener follows the motion from one "breath" to the next, although, as in Example 6.23, the lengths of these units are not predictable. What then is the difference between these two melodies? Though neither has a symmetrical phrase structure, the Gregorian Chant melody also lacks both a sense of meter and a sense of a compelling, directed melodic motion toward points of rest. The result is a melody which, despite its "breathing spaces," seems more continuous than sectional.

Examples 6.25–6.27 are even more continuous or cumulative in their effect. In the Bach aria (Example 6.25) the singer seems hardly to have an oppor-

| Example | Composer, Title | Date |
|---------|-----------------|------|
| 6.25 | Bach, *St. Matthew Passion,* aria | 1729 |
| 6.26 | Bach, *Partita 2,* gigue | c. 1720 |
| 6.27 | Wagner, *Tristan und Isolde,* excerpt from last act | 1857–1859 |

**6.25**  *"the melody moves continuously forward growing out of itself"*

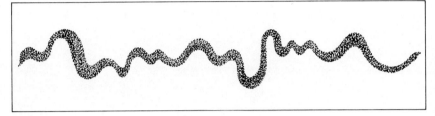

tunity to breathe. The melody moves continuously forward growing out of itself; there is no periodic phrase structure established by a series of related, regularly recurring goals. The effect is one of organic growth, a constant process of becoming.

While the Bach gigue (Example 6.26) is also continuous—after its two initial figures it unwinds in an almost never-ending series of runs—it nevertheless feels somewhat more regular in its organization. This feeling is a function of its many sequences. (*Sequence,* the repetition of the same melodic-rhythmic pattern at successively higher or lower pitch levels, is often a crucial organizing factor in continuously unwinding melodies.) The length of the sequential unit creates a structural rhythm of its own, since in the movement through each unit of the chain we feel a series of equal impulses. Composers can then influence the pace of the music by shortening or lengthening the sequential figures (Chapter 3, Additional Materials).

Finally, Example 6.27 from Wagner's *Tristan und Isolde* illustrates what the composer termed "end-

Pitch and
Movement

less melody" which, in a sense, has features of both cumulative and periodic melodic processes. The melody is shared jointly by soprano and orchestra. The soprano breathes, but the orchestra continues; through sequential development and extreme harmonic instability (when do you settle on a tonic?) the motion is continuous in a series of increasingly intense climaxes.

# ADDITIONAL MATERIALS

I

Examples 1–5 give you only the pitches of five familiar tunes; neither rhythmic shape nor meter (that is, bar lines) are indicated. Play the notes on the piano or some other instrument. For each example identify the melody and write it out with the correct rhythm and meter.

**Model Example**

**Solution (*Twinkle, Twinkle Little Star*)**

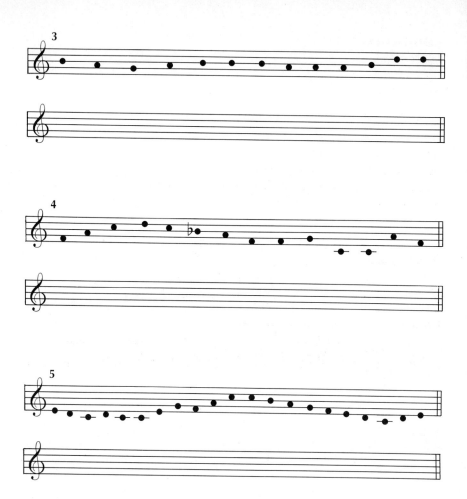

In Examples 6 and 7 you are given rhythmic configurations. Provide each rhythmic configuration with appropriate pitches.

**Model Example**

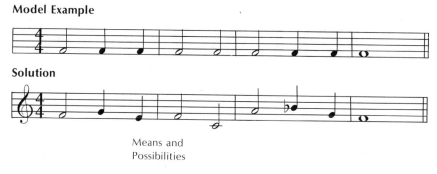

**Solution**

Means and
Possibilities

In Examples 8 and 9 you are given pitch shapes. Provide each pitch shape with an appropriate rhythmic shape.

**Model Example**

**Solution**

Pitch and
Movement

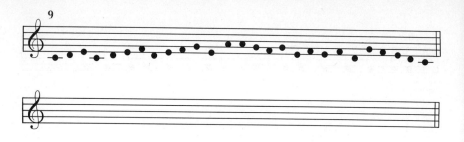

II

Study in detail some well-known tunes, trying to discover the fundamentals of their organization. Look, for example, for motives and their manipulation, melodic shape, phrases and the relationships among them (length, kind of cadence, and so on).

*Silent Night*
*Twinkle, Twinkle Little Star*
*Did You Ever See a Lassie?*
*Early One Morning*

III

Listen carefully to and study (as with the familiar tunes above) some more complex melodies.

Mozart, *Eine kleine Nachtmusik,* minuet, 1787
Schubert, songs from *Die Schöne Müllerin,* 1823: *Der Jäger* (see E2.2), *Des Müllers Blumen, Ungeduld* (see D6.14), and *Morgengruss*. Note, among other things, the readily apparent rhythmic patterns of the first three songs, compared with the almost speech-like quality and the much more subtle patterns of *Morgengruss*.

IV

Contrast, as examples of sectional and continuous

Means and
Possibilities

80

melodic organization, the opening melodies in the
following pieces:

Haydn, *Symphony 99,* third movement, 1793
Handel, *Concerto Grosso,* Opus 3, no. 1, first movement,
   c. 1734

Mozart, *Symphony 39,* fourth movement, 1788
Bach, *Brandenburg Concerto 5,* first movement, c. 1721


V

Listen to the composer's manipulation of motives,
on a larger scale, in the course of an entire movement.

Beethoven, *Symphony 5,* first movement, 1808 (One
   hears almost constant development of the opening
   four-note motive throughout the entire movement.
   It appears in a seemingly infinite variety of guises.)
Beethoven, *Quartet,* Opus 131, first movement, 1826
Schoenberg, *Pierrot lunaire,* Mondestrunken, 1912
Bach, *Well-Tempered Clavier,* Book I, C minor fugue,
   1722

# Structure:
# Process and
# Design

*The Enraged Musician*
William Hogarth, 1741
(Prints Division, The New York Public Library)

# MEANS OF ORGANIZATION 5

It might be well at this point to pause for a moment and reread Chapter 1 and listen again to Demonstration 1 in order to view what has happened thus far in your perception of music. You should find that we have reached a point at which we can begin to expand our focus. Those factors which we have of necessity temporarily isolated should now begin to merge. Analysis and terminology should assume their proper roles as means toward direct and immediate involvement in the total process of a work. Achieving this goal should justify, at least partially, the use of language which may at times have seemed more of a hindrance than a help.

Naming an object or a relationship—such as conjunct motion, sequence, dominant, or triple meter—often appears to interfere with your affective response, that is, your response to the feelings, character, and mood which music generates. It is interesting to read what Kurt Goldstein, a biological psychologist, has said concerning the connection between language (naming) and affect:

[Language] is not merely a superficial means of communication, not a simple naming of objects through words; it represents a particular way of building up the world—namely, by means of abstractions. . . . in none of his cultural creations does man reveal himself as fully as in the creation of language, itself.[1]

But a problem arises because:

If we try to become aware of them [feelings] we have to transform them into objects, and then their original character of attitudes, feelings, etc. is lost, and they are distorted into "things." . . . Thus, a phenomenon which is not experienced in a conscious form [feelings, attitudes, etc.] can never subsequently become directly conscious; and, conversely, a conscious phenomenon can never work directly upon attitudes or feelings. Only by way of the whole, by a detour, so to speak, can either influence, arouse, or disturb the other.[2]

These comments provide a broader framework which may help you to understand this moment in a process which may appear at this point to be a conglomeration of analytical bits and pieces rather than a total experience. We have tried to demonstrate, however, that an atomistic approach to the musical experience is, except as a temporary expedient, inadequate. Specifically, the concerns of Chapters 3 and 4 could not be kept separate; just as our discussion of rhythmic organization merged into one of melodic organization, so our discussion of melodic organization turned to rhythmic considerations. Henceforth, we will pursue more directly a holistic approach. Beginning with two exercises in which you are asked to discover some specific means through which composers create a sense of unity and variety in building whole structures, we move to a consideration of two fundamentally different approaches to creating these structures (Demonstration 7). Then we introduce the subject of harmony, which "more than any

[1] Kurt Goldstein, *Human Nature*, Schocken, New York, 1963, p. 83.
[2] *Ibid.*, pp. 152, 154.

Structure: Process
and Design

86

other musical element, brings to music the possibility of extension, or larger design";[3] and finally, incorporating all that has gone before, we move to a consideration of these "larger designs," concentrating on their varying effects.

[3] Roger Sessions, "The Composer and His Message," in Augusto Centeno, ed., *The Intent of the Artist,* Princeton, Princeton, N.J., 1941, p. 111.

Means of
Organization

## Exercise 2
## Return
## (side 7)

Exercise 2 asks you to discriminate between pieces following different structural procedures: those which include a return to the opening musical material and those which do not. To do so you will have to focus your attention for longer time spans, you will be considering musical events on a larger scale (with less detail), and you will be called upon to remember these events as the music proceeds. Remembering a musical event (or any event, for that matter) is often more successful if one "identifies" with its expressive character through an active involvement in it, rather than trying to remember its specific aspects, such as pitch or rhythmic configuration. A precise awareness of such specifics is extremely important when you are going deeply into a work, but at this point we are asking you to pause in your examination of details in order to consider larger design in one of its most general aspects: the difference between pieces in which you have the experience of returning after some kind of digression, and those in which your experience is one of continuing onward. (Note that in a number of the examples in Exercise 2 the composer has helped the listener to "fix" the initial event by repeating the opening section.)

As you listen, think not only about this fundamental difference in organization, but also, in those examples which include a return, about the differences in the way this return occurs. For example, is the return "announced"?—are you told musically that it is approaching? Or does it simply happen without any preparation? Notice, too, that in a number of instances the return is somewhat varied,

Structure: Process
and Design

although it still clearly projects the feeling of coming back after a contrasting middle section.

We have chosen to introduce an exercise rather than a demonstration at this point in order to encourage you to begin your own discovery of larger design. This is not a test. After you have completed the exercise, turn to the answers, where you will also find additional comments on some of the examples; we suggest that you listen to the examples again while reading these comments rather than simply checking to see if your answers are right or wrong. Listen carefully first to Examples 2.1 and 2.2 (for which answers are given); these can serve as models in doing the rest of the exercise.

| Example | No Return | Return |
|---------|-----------|--------|
| 2.1 |  | X |
| 2.2 | X |  |
| 2.3 |  |  |
| 2.4 |  |  |
| 2.5 |  |  |
| 2.6 |  |  |
| 2.7 |  |  |
| 2.8 |  |  |
| 2.9 |  |  |
| 2.10 |  |  |
| 2.11 |  |  |

Means of
Organization

## Correct Answers
## and Comments

| Example | Composer, Title | No Return | Return |
|---------|-----------------|-----------|--------|
| 2.1 | Mozart, *Horn Concerto 2*, K. 417, third movement, 1783 | | X |
| 2.2 | Schubert, *Die Schöne Müllerin*, Der Jäger, 1823 | X | |

The first two examples demonstrate the striking difference in effect that results from the fundamental difference in their structure: the feeling of coming back in Example 2.1 is clearly prepared for and emphasized by the trills and sustained note of the horn, in contrast to the impression of on-going movement without turning back which is felt in Example 2.2.

| | | | |
|---------|-----------------|-----------|--------|
| 2.3 | Bach, *Violin Concerto in E Major*, third movement, c. 1720 | | X |
| 2.4 | Bach, *Well-Tempered Clavier*, Book I, Prelude no. 2 in C Minor, 1722 | X | |

After listening to Example 2.3, with its clear sections, you cannot help but feel the tension created by the continuously progressing motion of Example 2.4. Thus two works by the same composer exemplify the different structural procedures under discussion.

| | | | |
|---------|-----------------|-----------|--------|
| 2.5 | Chopin, *Prelude*, Opus 28, no. 18, 1838 | X | |

Structure: Process
and Design

Compare the sense of continuously progressing movement in the Chopin prelude with that of Example 2.4.

| Example | Composer, Title | No Return | Return |
|---------|-----------------|-----------|--------|
| 2.6 | Beethoven, *Sonata for Violin and Piano,* Opus 30, no. 2, scherzo, 1802 | | X |
| 2.7 | Binchois, *De plus en plus,* c. 1450 | | X |
| 2.8 | Haydn, *Symphony 96,* fourth movement, 1791 | | X |

While Binchois simply starts over again (though with different text) after the middle section, Haydn has a grand time playing around with your anticipation of a return.

| | | | |
|---------|-----------------|-----------|--------|
| 2.9 | Stravinsky, *Petrouchka,* 1911 | | X |
| 2.10 | Webern, *Five Pieces for Orchestra,* Opus 10, no. 2, 1913 | X | |
| 2.11 | Bizet, *Symphony in C,* third movement, 1855 | X | |

Notice that in Example 2.11 one is led to expect a return. As in many of the other examples in which there were returns, the first part is repeated; in addition there is a long preparation. Instead of a return, however, new material is introduced.

## Exercise 3
## Motivic Repetition
## (side 7)

The previous exercise (which dealt with return) illustrated a fundamental aspect of musical organization—the melding of *unity* and *variety*—as exemplified in the large dimensions of pieces, namely, by a statement, followed by a digression of some length, and finally a return. On the most general level, then, unity was achieved through return (repetition), variety through digression (contrast). This exercise is also concerned with repetition and contrast, but in smaller dimensions—that is, on a level of much greater detail. We deal here not with large sections, but with the *motive*, the pattern of tones that one perceives as the smallest structural unit, and from which larger structures are generated (see also Chapters 3 and 4). We are concerned with various means by which composers may manipulate motives in order to move the piece along from moment to moment, in the process achieving both unity (by maintaining aspects of the motive) and variety (by altering aspects of the motive).

While we have dealt with the motivic aspect of music in the discussion of particular melodies (in Demonstration 6), the examples in this exercise illustrate three specific procedures—sequence, imitation, and literal repetition—which composers have used in treating the motive as a basis for larger musical development.

The examples you will hear illustrate several procedures or devices through which motives may be manipulated. However, it is not your ability simply to identify these techniques that is important. Rather, it is that through the discovery of specific musical details you come closer to an understanding of and involvement with the larger musical

Structure: Process
and Design

design and expressiveness of works in which such compositional devices play an active role.

The first four examples—remarkably different in effect—show the procedures which you are asked to listen for as you fill in the table on page 95.

Example 3.1: *Repetition by sequence.* Repetition of a melodic pattern (motive) at successively higher or lower pitch levels within the *same strand* of the texture constitutes a sequence (see Chapter 4). In this example there are two consecutive sequences.

**Example 3.1**

Example 3.2: *Repetition by imitation.* The motive is tossed around, generating a rhythmically active texture as it appears successively *in different parts.*

A motive is stated at the beginning, then other
instruments enter with it at different pitch levels.
Notice that the pacing of the successive entries

**Example 3.2**

Structure: Process
and Design

contributes to the higher-level rhythmic structure of the piece (see Demonstration 3).

Example 3.3: *Literal repetition.* A three-note motive is literally repeated, after which a second repetition is extended to complete the phrase. The whole passage is then immediately repeated at a higher pitch level. The effect is strikingly different from that of Examples 1 and 2; while these examples proceed immediately forward from their initial "cell" statements, Example 3 seems at first to be "stuck," motionless, until it moves on. (Such

| Example | A<br>Sequence | B<br>Imitation | C<br>Literal | D<br>None |
|---|---|---|---|---|
| 3.1 | X | | | |
| 3.2 | | X | | |
| 3.3 | | | X | |
| 3.4 | | | | X |
| 3.5 | | | | |
| 3.6 | | | | |
| 3.7 | | | | |
| 3.8 | | | | |
| 3.9 | | | | |
| 3.10 | | | | |
| 3.11 | | | | |
| 3.12 | | | | |
| 3.13 | | | | |
| 3.14 | | | | |
| 3.15 | | | | |
| 3.16 | | | | |
| 3.17 | | | | |

Means of
Organization

literal repetition of a motive is used sometimes at the end of a section to reinforce the conclusion.)

Example 3.4: *None of the above.* Notice the difference in the effect of this melody, in which there is no motivic repetition (neither sequence, imitation, nor literal repetition), compared with the previous examples, in which a single motive was the fundamental building block for a passage. This melody has a more free-floating, amorphous character.

Listen carefully to the first four examples; then fill in the rest of the table on page 95, matching each excerpt with the appropriate letter.

A. Sequence.
B. Imitation.
C. Literal repetition.
D. None of the above.

*Correct Answers*
*and Comments*

| Example | Composer, Title | A Sequence | B Imitation | C Literal | D None |
|---------|-----------------|------------|-------------|-----------|--------|
| 3.1 | Vivaldi, *Concerto,* Opus 3, no. 7, c. 1712 | X | | | |
| 3.2 | A. Gabrieli, *Ricercare,* c. 1580 | | X | | |
| 3.3 | Brahms, *Rhapsodie,* Opus 79, no. 1, 1879 | | | X | |
| 3.4 | *Gaudete Populi* (Mozarabic chant) | | | | X |
| 3.5 | Palestrina, *Missa In festis Apostolorum,* Kyrie, c. 1580 | | X | | |

Structure: Process
and Design

| Example | Composer, Title | *A* Sequence | *B* Imitation | *C* Literal | *D* None |
|---------|-----------------|--------------|---------------|-------------|----------|
| 3.6 | Vivaldi, *Concerto,* Opus 3, no. 3, c. 1712 | X | | | |
| 3.7 | R. Strauss, *Till Eulenspiegel,* 1895 | | | X | |
| 3.8 | Schubert, *Piano Sonata in B♭,* 1828 | X | | | |

In Example 3.8, the sequential passage follows a rather long section in which there is no melodic repetition of the kind defined in this exercise. Notice the difference between the freely flowing, suspenseful opening and the clearly directed sequential passage which follows it.

| 3.9 | Mendelssohn, *Piano Concerto in G Minor,* 1831 | | | X | |
|-----|-----|-----|-----|-----|-----|

Example 3.9 includes the literal repetition of three different motives. The composer treats the first motive like those given in Examples 3.3 and 3.7, that is, two statements plus a third which is extended. The other two motives are repeated only once.

| 3.10 | Bach, *Cantata 21, Ich hatte viel Bekümmernis,* 1714 | | X | | |
|------|-----|-----|-----|-----|-----|
| 3.11 | Hindemith, *Mathis der Maler,* 1934 | | X | | |

Means of
Organization

| Example | Composer, Title | A Sequence | B Imitation | C Literal | D None |
|---------|-----------------|------------|-------------|-----------|--------|
| 3.12 | Haydn, *Symphony 97*, first movement, 1792 | | | | X |
| 3.13 | Schoenberg, *Suite, for Piano,* Opus 25, gavotte, 1925 | X | | | |
| 3.14 | Vivaldi, *Concerto,* Opus 3, no. 11, c. 1712 | X | | | |

Notice the striking difference in effect between the sequential passages of Examples 3.13 and 3.14. This difference stems from the quality of the motives themselves as well as from the role of the sequence in the process of the piece. The regularity of a sequence is unexpected in the rapidly changing complexity of Schoenberg, while it is a normative procedure for Vivaldi.

| | | | | | |
|---------|-----------------|------------|-------------|-----------|--------|
| 3.15 | Weill, *The Rise and Fall of the City of Mahagonny,* 1930 | X | | X | |

Literal repetition of a motive occurs at the beginning of the excerpt, and the shortened motive is then treated sequentially—all before the voices enter.

| | | | | | |
|---------|-----------------|------------|-------------|-----------|--------|
| 3.16 | Stravinsky, *Octet for Wind Instruments* (see D6.13), 1923–1924 | | | | X |

Structure: Process
and Design

| Example | Composer, Title | A Sequence | B Imitation | C Literal | D None |
|---------|-----------------|------------|-------------|-----------|--------|
| 3.17 | Bizet, *Symphony in C*, 1855 | | | X | |

Example 3.17 shows literal motivic repetition which reinforces the conclusion of the piece.

Means of
Organization

Sectional and
Continuous
Organization
(side 8)

This demonstration is an introduction to the study of large-scale structure in music. While aspects of structure have been touched on previously,[4] we have not yet focused on the overall organization of a piece. You will hear in this demonstration a number of short pieces (the majority of them complete) which have been chosen to illustrate two fundamentally different approaches to larger musical design: (1) pieces which one hears immediately as divided into parts, whether or not they include return (*sectional*), and (2) pieces which one cannot easily divide into parts (*continuous*). By *parts* we refer now not to the smaller units defined by caesurae, but rather to those larger significant structural units which lend themselves to schematic representation. (These large parts may be designated A, B, C, and so forth.)

I

| Example | Composer, Title | Date |
|---------|-----------------|------|
| 7.1 | Mozart, *German Dance*, K. 605, no. 1 | 1791 |
| 7.2 | Chopin, *Prelude*, Opus 28, no. 18 | 1838 |

Examples 7.1 and 7.2 should make the fundamental distinction clear. Example 7.1 by Mozart, a typical

[4]See Chapter 2, Additional Materials, sonority and texture as organizing factors; Chapter 3, rhythm (beat, meter, phrase, sequence) as an organizing factor; Chapter 4, melodic organization; Exercises 2 and 3, return and repetition.

Structure: Process
and Design

late eighteenth-century dance, is clearly divided into three sections. Its structure is conventionally represented as follows: first section, A; second section (because of its new material), B; and then a return, A' (a somewhat abbreviated version of A)—thus, ABA'. Each of these three sections is "closed out," relatively complete in itself. Both A and B can be heard as ||:a:||:b + a':||. (The symbol ||:    :|| indicates that the music between the signs is to be played again.) Notice that b and a' flow into one another more than B and A'. (Thus it is labeled b + a' rather than b a'.) What other differ-

a               b + a'

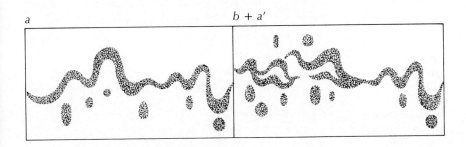

ences do you hear between the ABA' structure and the a b + a' structure, and what differences do you hear among the smaller parts—a, b, and a'?

**7.2** *"the Chopin prelude cannot be divided into parts"*

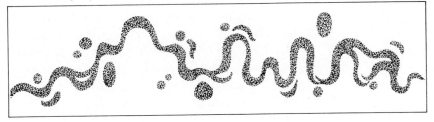

In contrast, the Chopin prelude (Example 7.2) cannot be divided into parts—it moves continuously forward *in spite of the caesurae or "breathing" pauses.*

Means of
Organization

II

| Example | Composer, Title | Date |
|---------|-----------------|------|
| 7.3 | Schubert, *Ländler*, Opus 171, no. 4 | 1823 |
| 7.4 | Mozart, *Variations on "Ah, vous dirai-je, Maman,"* K. 265 | 1778 |

The next two examples, like Example 7.1, are both sectional, yet each is organized differently. The Schubert dance (Example 7.3) is in two clear sections—||:A:||:B:||. Each part is repeated, but there is no return. (What sort of relationship is there between A and B?) The Mozart piece (Example 7.4) is a theme with variations (not all of which are included). The theme, itself, is sectional— ||:a:||:b + a':||—and each of the three variations given follows the same scheme. The theme and

**7.4** *"a theme with variations"*

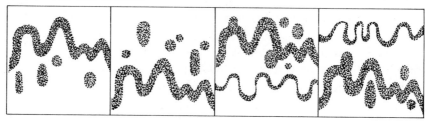

each variation on it are separate and distinct entities. (What differentiates one variation from another?) The result is a work that might be described as additive; each large section (variation) is added on to the previous one, and all of them together make up a particular kind of whole.

III

Examples 7.5–7.7 are all organized so as to create a continuous structure, but one listens to each of them rather differently. The Renaissance piece by

Structure: Process
and Design

| Example | Composer, Title | Date |
|---------|-----------------|------|
| 7.5 | Palestrina, *Missa In festis Apostolorum*, Kyrie | c. 1580 |
| 7.6 | Bach, *Two-Part Invention in F Major*, no. 8 | c. 1720 |
| 7.7 | Froberger, *Toccata 2* | c. 1650 |

Palestrina (Example 7.5) is active in texture; the parts enter in imitation and are rhythmically independent (see E3.5). Thus, the effect is one of unceasing movement characterized by melodic homogeneity. There is, however, a contrast in tone color as well as an increase in textural density as the parts pile up on top of one another. The Bach invention (Example 7.6) is also active in texture, but this time, since there are only two "voices," the texture is thinner throughout. Like the previous example the piece begins with imitation; unlike it, however, there is a clear point of arrival a little less than halfway through the piece. Example 7.7 has a quality of improvisation, with its elided sections [slow–fast (imitative)–slow] creating changes of mood. One might represent its structure as ABA' (with the B section dividing into *bb'*), but the proportions of the sections (the middle being the largest), the manner in which they run into one another, and the lack of lower-level sectionality (clear phrase structure) make such a schematic representation almost meaningless as compared with the diagram of Example 7.1.

IV

| Example | Composer, Title | Date |
|---------|-----------------|------|
| 7.8 | Rameau, *Suite in E*, gigue no. 2 | 1724 |
| 7.9 | Haydn, *Trio in G*, Rondo all' Ongarese | 1791 |

Examples 7.8 and 7.9 are again sectional. Unlike the Froberger organ toccata, they can be meaningfully diagrammed—that is, a diagram will represent the progress of the piece and the perceived relationships among the parts. Rameau's piece (Example 7.8) can be thought of as having a refrain (A), the entire gigue proceeding as follows: ABACADA. (How do the various sections differ? Are they each in themselves relatively sectional or continuous?) The Haydn trio (Example 7.9) is similar in procedure, although it is much more extended in each of its parts, and consequently much longer. It may be diagrammed as ABACA Coda, but—unlike Ex-

**7.9**  *"a rondo"*

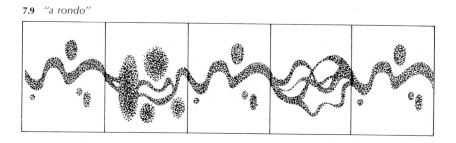

ample 7.8—each of its parts is further subdivided into two or more smaller parts. The type of structural procedure illustrated by Examples 7.8 and 7.9 is called a *rondo*.

V

The last four examples are all continuous in their organization. The Chopin prelude (Example 7.2 above) is repeated here as Example 7.10 for comparison with the stylistically different Schoenberg piece (Example 7.11). Both have a continuously onward impulse despite clear caesurae. The Bach aria, part of which is given as Example 7.12, was heard previously as D6.25, where it was char-

| Example | Composer, Title | Date |
|---------|-----------------|------|
| 7.10 | Chopin, *Prelude,* Opus 28, no. 18 | 1838 |
| 7.11 | Schoenberg, *Six Little Piano Pieces,* Opus 19, no. 4 | 1911 |
| 7.12 | Bach, *St. Matthew Passion,* aria | 1729 |
| 7.13 | Stravinsky, *Le Sacre du printemps,* beginning | 1913 |

acterized as follows: "The melody moves continuously forward growing out of itself; there is no periodic phrase structure established by a series of related, regularly recurring goals. The effect is one of organic growth, a constant process of becoming."

While we were speaking earlier of only one aspect of organization, melody, you can now hear how a continuous melody tends to generate a continuous structure, which is further reinforced by homogeneity of texture and singleness of theme.

Example 7.13 is paradoxically static and in motion at the same time. Changes in sonority and texture (the piling up of sound beginning with the solo bassoon, for example) create a sense of kaleidoscopic motion, yet a motion that is inhibited by the persistence of a few melodic and rhythmic fragments.

## ADDITIONAL
## MATERIALS

The examples in Demonstration 7 were chosen primarily as illustrations of the fundamental difference between sectional and continuous structure. It is important now to consider a few examples more deeply in order to perceive the individual aspects of a few works and at the same time become aware of some further general aspects of musical design. Consider the following questions carefully in relation to all the works in this section.

1. Does the piece divide into larger sections which are readily perceived?
2. Within these larger sections, is the structure basically sectional or continuous?
3. What defines or marks off sections?
4. What is the relationship among sections?
5. What are the sources of contrast? of unity?

I

Listen to the following two pieces, both of which were included in Demonstration 7 (Examples 7.3 and 7.6):

Schubert, *Ländler*, Opus 171, no. 4, 1823
Bach, *Two-Part Invention in F Major*, no. 8, c. 1720

In Demonstration 7 Schubert's work illustrated a sectional piece; Bach's illustrated a continuous one. The two pieces do have a superficial similarity in structure: each reaches a point of arrival, a caesura which divides it into two parts. However, they operate on fundamentally different structural principles. Schubert's texture is *homophonic* (consisting of a melody and accompaniment) and it proceeds in clear, four-measure phrases—two phrases in Part A, two in Part B—creating two equal halves. The relationship between the first two phrases is rather different than the one that exists between the second two: the first two are essentially antecedent–consequent in relationship. What generates the sense of tension in the third phrase, and why do we have almost a sense of return—at least return to stability—in the concluding phrase? Bach's invention, on the other hand, is a *polyphonic* piece which begins imitatively and continues with an active texture in which the two parts, though similar melodically, retain their rhythmic independence throughout. This rhythmic independence does not allow for the kind of clear, balanced phrase structure heard in the Schubert (which defined the *Ländler* as sectional). Why? The continuous flow is finally interrupted with a caesura (not, however, exactly at the midpoint, where it came in Schubert's piece, but only one-third of the way through). Following the caesura, the opening imitation reappears, but not in the tonic key of the piece and without a strong sense of return to the opening—it is merely another phase in the continuous development of the initial figure. (Can you hear how Bach exploits motives from that figure in the course of the piece?) The last portion of the invention is exactly the same (except in a different key) as the part before the caesura, yet one does not hear this repetition as a return. Why?

II

Listen to and compare the following two pieces, the first of which was also included in Demonstration 7 (Example 7.1).

Mozart, *German Dance*, K. 605, no. 1, 1791
Haydn, *Symphony 99*, third movement, 1793

The Mozart dance (D7.1) served to illustrate an ABA' structure. In turn A and B were divided into ||:a:||:b + a':||, while A' was the same as A without repeats. The Haydn minuet could be schematically diagrammed in exactly the same way, yet it is a much larger, more imposing work. What happens within A and B to sustain the greatly expanded proportions? Notice, for example, that while the *a* section of the *German Dance* was a simple two-phrase, antecedent–consequent statement, the *a* section of the Haydn minuet is only one-third complete at the end of its opening antecedent–consequent statement—it continues on to a section which generates more tension and ends with a closing passage which is more stable. What causes these differences in effect? How does *b* differ from *a*, how is the return to *a'* effected, and what surprising events occur in this return? A careful study of the Haydn minuet should give you an appreciation of its composer's genius in generating out of very simple musical material a work filled with contrasts: a dance, suspense, humor, climax, all making a tightly packed, eminently satisfying whole.

III

Palestrina, *Missa Aeterna Christi munera*, Sanctus, 1590

This movement from a sixteenth-century setting of the Mass is continuous throughout, without any obvious breaks in the musical flow. But careful listening will reveal the existence of four "sections" marked off by carefully concealed points of arrival. In this polyphonic piece the text is a significant structural determinant, for a new series of imitative entries occurs with each line of text: (1) "Sanctus," (2) "Dominus Deus . . . ," (3) "Pleni sunt coeli

Structure: Process
and Design

. . . ," and (4) "Hosanna . . . ." What musical elements create the "section" boundaries? How are these points concealed?


IV

Schubert, *Impromptu,* Opus 90, no. 2, c. 1827
Chopin, *Prelude,* Opus 28, no. 18, 1838 (see D7.2)
Schoenberg, *Six Little Piano Pieces,* Opus 19, no. 4, 1911
    (see D7.11)


Focus on the A section of the ABA Schubert impromptu. The melody is a series of rapidly flowing notes which seem never to stop—there is no caesura in this upper part of the texture. But would the piece be accurately described as continuous? No, but why not? The answer lies in the very clear balanced phrase structure adumbrated by the left-hand accompaniment. Compared to this piece, the Chopin prelude seems, on the most immediate level, very discontinuous, proceeding in fits and starts. Yet, the overall impression is that the music never really stops at the breaks—that it synaptically flows onward until the final cadence. Why? (The primary reason is harmonic.) Finally, as was pointed out in Demonstration 7, despite the stylistic (and chronological) differences between the Schoenberg piece and the Chopin prelude, there are some striking similarities between them. Both have a rhythmic and metric freedom which gives them an almost improvisatory air; both grow unceasingly out of the initial motivic material, which undergoes almost magical transformation.


V

The following are large complex pieces, a detailed discussion of which would require many pages.

Listen to them on your own, for they will provide invaluable experience in coming to grips with extensive pieces. Ask the five questions listed above for each piece.

Purcell, *Dido and Aeneas,* Dido's lament, 1689
Wagner, *Tristan und Isolde,* prelude, 1857–1859
Handel, *Concerto Grosso,* Opus 3, no. 1, c. 1734
Mozart, *Piano Sonata in F,* K. 332, first movement, 1778

*Madame Favart*
François Hubert Drouais, 1757
(The Metropolitan Museum of Art, New York; The Mr. and Mrs.
Isaac D. Fletcher Collection; bequest of Isaac D. Fletcher, 1917)

# HARMONY

Demonstration 8

Harmony:
The Building Blocks
(side 9)

*Harmony* is traditionally defined as the relationship among chords. A *chord* results from the sounding together of two or more tones. Chords, as entities considered in themselves, evolved from the simultaneous sounding of independently moving "voices"; in effect, they are a vertical slicing-through of the texture. Harmony also can be considered as the framework of a given piece, and *tonal harmony*—sometimes called *functional harmony*—as that framework within which composers worked from roughly 1650 to 1900. This demonstration will introduce you to the fundamental chord relationships which define tonal harmony and provide the foundations of tonality.

The discussion is rudimentary in at least two senses. (1) It deals with only the most "primitive" (and basic) tools of tonal harmony—the triad and its three most essential functions within a given key: tonic, dominant, and subdominant, or I, V, and IV. (2) It deals with simple melodies and demonstrates their equally simple harmonic structure.

You will observe that the discussion concentrates on encouraging you to make discriminations of an extremely detailed, perhaps overly discrete, sort, particularly in the perception of changes from one chord and its function to another. It should be remembered that this is not the kind of activity with which one is involved in listening to a piece of music; the examples should be studied as one studies molecular biology in relation to physiology, with the confidence that in both cases the study of "bits" leads eventually to a better understanding of the functioning of a total organism. Specifically, the ability to hear the motion from the I chord to the V chord should lead not only to a better understanding of harmony on the conceptual level, but, more important, to a more adequate perception of *harmonic functions* on a larger scale, such as the harmonic stability or instability of a given passage and the role of harmony in creating structure and various kinds of affect within an entire work. It is to these latter matters that we will turn our attention in Demonstrations 9 and 10.

The basic discussion of harmony is on the record itself. Below you will find some definitions and examples to which you may refer while listening.

*Triad:*   A chord made up of three tones. The lowest tone is called the *root* of the chord, derived from the notion of a single tone, or root, out of which the chord grows or evolves. A triad can be built on any note of the scale by adding to that tone those which lie a third and a fifth above it in the scale. Thus, the tonic triad (or I) has as its root the tonic note, and above it the third and fifth degrees of the scale; the dominant triad (or V) has as its

**Example 1**    (in the Key of C)

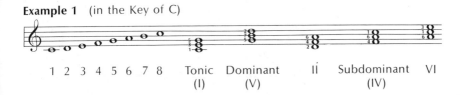

1  2  3  4  5  6  7  8      Tonic    Dominant        II      Subdominant    VI
                  (I)          (V)                              (IV)

root the fifth degree of the scale and above it the seventh and second degrees. (See the Ancillary Reading section for further information.)

*Inversion:*   A rearrangement of the notes of a triad so that the root is no longer the lowest note.

**Example 2**    (Inversions of II in C Major)

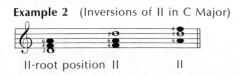

II-root position  II                    II

*Arpeggio* or broken chord:   An arpeggio consists of playing the notes of a triad one after the other through one or more octaves.

**Example 3**

For Examples 4 and 7, the harmonic implications of a melody, as realized in its accompaniment, are demonstrated on the record.

Note that in Example 4, although the seventh degree is not in the melody, the syntactical framework, the tonality, is still clear.

Harmony

115

**Example 4**

Scale degrees:

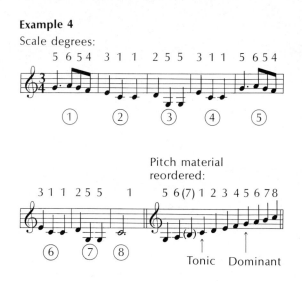

*Transposition:* The process of rewriting a melody using a different collection of pitches (and thus establishing a different tonal center) while keeping the *successive relationships* of the pitches the same.

**Example 5**

Scale degrees:

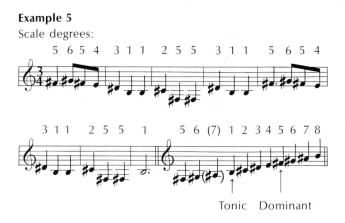

In actually writing the melody shown in Example 4 in B Major the sharps would be assimilated into the key signature as in Example 6.

Structure: Process
and Design

**Example 6**

**Example 7**

Scale degrees:

Notice that the I chord in G (Example 8) is the same as the V chord in C (Example 1); the IV chord in G is the same as I in C. Thus, the two keys a fifth apart are very closely related, having two fundamental chords in common—although these chords have different functions in relation to their tonics. Composers play with these possibilities, moving easily from one key to the other or even setting up an ambiguity between them.

**Example 8**

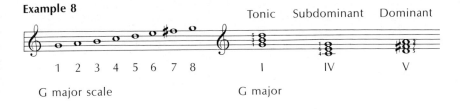

Tonic    Subdominant    Dominant

1  2  3  4  5  6  7  8            I            IV            V

G major scale                G major

Harmony

117

*Full cadence:* The dominant harmony moves to the tonic harmony at the end of a phrase, as shown at the end of Example 9.

*Half cadence:* The dominant harmony is used at the end of a phrase, as at the end of the first phrase in Example 9. See also the discussion of phrase structure and cadences in Chapter 4.

**Example 9**

Scale degrees:

Half cadence          Full cadence

**Example 10** ("Jesu, nun sei gepreiset")

**Exercise 4**
**Major–Minor; I and V**
**(side 12)**

This exercise has a somewhat different purpose
from that of Exercises 2 and 3. The earlier exercises
were intended as initial steps toward your discovery of structure as such; this exercise, coming
after you have had some experience with musical
organization (through examination of return, repetition, sectional and continuous structure, and harmony) is intended simply to give you practice in
hearing three rather specific elements which are
part of musical syntax: major–minor distinctions,
full and half cadences, and chord progressions
involving I and V.

We emphasize once more that this is *only* an
exercise; completing it successfully should be considered not a significant achievement in itself, but
rather a contribution to your later musical involvement.

I

In Chapter 4 and its Ancillary Reading (p. 299) there
was some discussion of the difference between the
major and minor modes. It was pointed out there
that the essential difference between the two
modes lies in the third degree of the scale; that
is, while the third degree is a *major* third above
the tonic (two whole steps) in the major mode,
it is a *minor* third above the tonic (a whole step
plus a half step) in the minor mode. Or, putting
it more simply, the third degree of the scale is a
half step closer to the tonic in the minor mode
than it is in the major mode. The tonic *triad,* which
involves this third degree, is therefore also different
in major and minor. In the Ancillary Reading for

**TONIC TRIAD IN C MAJOR**     **TONIC TRIAD IN C MINOR**

Chapters 4 and 6 the various forms of minor scales are given as well as the resultant triads.

The following exercises will give you some practice in distinguishing between pieces in the major and minor modes. While pieces in major or minor do, indeed, sound different, no rules can be given for acquiring the ability to distinguish between them; we might compare the problem to finding rules for distinguishing between blue and yellow. (In a sense, the difference between major and minor is like a change in the color of a tonality, for it is not a change in the key, the tonal center itself.) Learning to distinguish between colors or between modes comes basically from experience and practice—in the case of the modes it is a useful but not crucial ability.

Listen to each example, now, and determine whether the piece is in major or minor, or whether it changes from one to the other during its course. (The answers are given following Part II.)

| Example | Major | Minor | Major → Minor | Minor → Major |
|---------|-------|-------|---------------|---------------|
| 4.1     |       |       |               |               |
| 4.2     |       |       |               |               |
| 4.3     |       |       |               |               |
| 4.4     |       |       |               |               |
| 4.5     |       |       |               |               |
| 4.6     |       |       |               |               |
| 4.7     |       |       |               |               |

Structure: Process
and Design

II

*Problem I:*   To discriminate between half cadences (dominant harmony) and full cadences (tonic harmony).

*Problem II:*   To discriminate between the tonic and dominant chords as they occur within a phrase.

*Method:*   Each example presents one phrase or two closely linked phrases (the latter are indicated). Do Problem I first, then go through the examples again answering Problem II.

*Problem I:*   Listen to the phrase and determine whether it ends with a full cadence or a half cadence.

*Problem II:*

1. Follow the diagram of the example, making sure that you can hear the grouping of beats into measures as indicated. The notes written into the measures refer only to the *beats* in each measure, not to the rhythm of the melody or the accompaniment.
2. Listen for the changes of harmony from I to V or V to I.
3. Write in each measure the numerals I or V, indicating the chord which harmonizes that measure. There will be only one *harmony* per measure.

## Problem I

| Example | A Tonic (Full Cadence) | B Dominant (Half Cadence) |
|---------|:----------------------:|:-------------------------:|
| 4.8 | X | |
| 4.9 | | X |
| 4.10 | | |
| 4.11 | | |
| 4.12 | | |
| 4.13 | | |
| 4.14[a] | | |
| 4.15 | | |
| 4.16 | | |
| 4.17[a] | | |
| 4.18 | | |
| 4.19 | | |
| 4.20[a] | | |

[a] These three examples have two phrases each. Consider the cadence of the second phrase only.

Structure: Process
and Design

## Problem II

| Example | Composer, Title[a] | Major | Minor | Major → Minor | Minor → Major |
|---------|--------------------|-------|-------|---------------|---------------|
| 4.1 | | | X | | |
| 4.2 | | | X | | |
| 4.3 | Mozart, *Sonata,* K. 331, 1778 | X | | | |
| 4.4 | Mozart, *Sonata,* K. 331, 1778 | | X | | |
| 4.5 | Schubert, *Allegretto in C,* 1816 | | | X | |
| 4.6 | Mozart, *Quartet,* K. 421, 1783 | | | | X |
| 4.7 | Schubert, *Die Winterreise,* Der Lindenbaum, 1827 | | | X | |

[a] Examples 4.1, 4.2, and 4.8 to 4.13 were prepared by the authors specifically for this exercise.

Structure: Process
and Design

*Problem I*                                    *Problem II*

| Example | Composer, Title | A | B |
|---|---|---|---|
| 4.8 | | X | |
| 4.9 | | | X |
| 4.10 | | | X |
| 4.11 | | X | |
| 4.12 | | X | |
| 4.13 | | X | |
| 4.14[a] | Beethoven, *Ländler*, no. 4, 1798 | X | |
| 4.15 | Beethoven, *Ländler*, no. 5, 1798 | X | |
| 4.16 | Beethoven, *Minuet in G*, 1795 | X | |
| 4.17[a] | Haydn, *Symphony 97*, third movement (trio), 1792 | X | |
| 4.18 | Haydn, *Symphony 94*, third movement, 1791 | | X |
| 4.19 | Haydn, *Symphony 100*, third movement, 1794 | | X |
| 4.20[a] | Beethoven, *Septet*, Opus 20, 1800 | X | |

*Problem II*

| Meter | | | | | | | | |
|---|---|---|---|---|---|---|---|---|
| $\frac{2}{4}$ | I | I | V | I | | | | |
| $\frac{6}{8}$ | I | I | V | V | | | | |
| $\frac{3}{4}$ | I | V | I | V | | | | |
| $\frac{2}{4}$ | I | V | V | I | | | | |
| $\frac{3}{4}$ | I | I | V | I | | | | |
| $\frac{4}{4}$ | V | I | V | I | | | | |
| $\frac{3}{4}$ | I | I | V | V | I | I | V | I |
| $\frac{3}{4}$ | V | I | V | I | V | I | V | I |
| $\frac{3}{4}$ | I | I | V | I | | | | |
| $\frac{3}{4}$ | I | I | V | V | V | I | V | I |
| $\frac{3}{4}$ | I | I | V | V | | | | |
| $\frac{3}{4}$ | I | I | V | V | | | | |
| $\frac{3}{4}$ | V | I | V | I | V | I | V | I |

[a] These examples illustrate an antecedent-consequent phrase relationship.

Harmony

We are primarily concerned in this demonstration with harmonic means as they serve various structural functions. For example, we will consider harmonic relationships which generate a sense of stability—the use of chords from only one "family of pitches" (one key), primarily I, IV, and V, to create a clear tonal center. At the same time we will consider harmonic relationships which generate a sense of instability through the use of chromaticism (a mixing of several families of pitches) to create an ambiguous or a shifting tonal center. We will also make a distinction between tension created by an ambiguous or shifting tonality, and *directed* tension created by a prolonged dominant harmony within one key.

Two pieces will be discussed in great detail so that you may become aware of the relationship between specific harmonic tools and their concomitant effects. The written material requires very close reading and, more important, the analysis demands that you listen very closely to the music. You will probably want to go back and play the examples a number of times.

I

| Example | Composer, Title | Date |
|---------|-----------------|------|
| 9.1 | Haydn, *Symphony 97,* third movement, trio | 1792 |
| 9.2 |    *a* section of trio | |
| 9.3 |    *a* repeated and *b* section | |
| 9.4 |    *b* section of trio | |
| 9.5 |    entire trio | |

Demonstration 8 was devoted to the rudiments of harmony and essentially to the harmonization of melodies. Now we must go on to consider larger works in which the statement of a melody is merely a beginning. Listen now to Example 9.1.

From our previous discussions, you will have observed that this portion of the symphony is sectional—it has a clear ||:a:||:b + a':|| structure. Here, however, the repeats of a and of b + a' are not literal but are slightly varied by changes in orchestration. Our question now is, following the statements of a, how is the b section defined or generated? What creates contrast and, specifically, what role does harmony play in creating this contrast?

Like the simple tunes discussed in Demonstration 8, the a section of this trio is harmonized with only the I and V chords. The harmony of the first two phrases in shown in Diagram 1. You may remember the example from Exercise 4 (E4.17).

**Diagram 1**

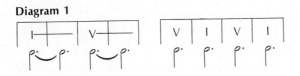

In Example 9.2 the harmony moves simply from the tonic to the dominant in the first phrase, and from dominant back to tonic in the second phrase. Notice that the *harmonic rhythm*—the rate at which the harmony moves or changes—speeds up in the second phrase: one chord for two bars in Phrase 1, and one chord for each bar in Phrase 2. There are thus two balanced phrases, one moving away from the tonic and ending with a half cadence (dominant), and the other moving back to the tonic and ending with a full cadence (tonic).

Turn now to Example 9.3. Note the varied orchestration in the repeat of *a;* then consider how the harmony in *b* differs from that of *a*. While *b* is the same length as *a* (eight measures), we do not hear *b* as a thematic statement. The melodic material of *b* is closely related to that of *a*, but in *b* it becomes more continuous: it no longer has the clear, balanced phrase structure of *a*, and consequently does not function as thematic statement.

How does harmony contribute to these differences? It was clear that the "balanced" (almost rocking) harmony of *a* contributed to its balanced, clear phrase structure. $\boxed{\text{I} \longrightarrow \text{V}}$ $\boxed{\text{V} \longrightarrow \text{I}}$ In *b* the harmony and the bass note remain fixed on the dominant $\boxed{\text{V} \longrightarrow \qquad}$ contributing to its athematic, continuous character. Thus on one level *b* has a single, dominant harmonic function, but on a more detailed level, the harmony

**TABLE 1**

|  | *a* | *b* |
| --- | --- | --- |
| *Affect:* | Stability | Less directed followed by more directed tension |
| *Means:* | Clear, balanced phrase structure; regular basic (I and V) harmony | More continuous melody; underlying static harmony (dominant pedal); harmonic movement within harmonic stasis |
| *Structural function:* | Thematic statement | Digression: development followed by waiting |

Structure: Process
and Design

hints at the dominant becoming itself a tonic, only to lead back to *a* and the real tonic once more. Procedures in *b*, then, are quite different from those in *a*. Listen to the *b* section alone (Example 9.4). The comparison between *a* and *b* is summarized in Table 1.

Following *b*, we return to the stability of thematic statement: *a* returns varied only by instrumentation. Listen again to the whole trio (Example 9.5). Its skeletal structure is given in Diagram 2.

**Diagram 2**

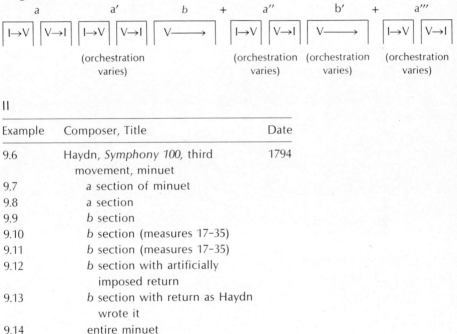

| Example | Composer, Title | Date |
|---------|-----------------|------|
| 9.6 | Haydn, *Symphony 100*, third movement, minuet | 1794 |
| 9.7 | a section of minuet | |
| 9.8 | a section | |
| 9.9 | b section | |
| 9.10 | b section (measures 17–35) | |
| 9.11 | b section (measures 17–35) | |
| 9.12 | b section with artificially imposed return | |
| 9.13 | b section with return as Haydn wrote it | |
| 9.14 | entire minuet | |

Continuing now in the process of considering harmonic functions and structure in ever larger and more complex works, listen to the minuet from Haydn's *Symphony 100* (Example 9.6). The score is printed in the following pages.

F. J. HAYDN

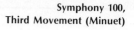

MENUETTO
Moderato

**b,** Phase 1

20   Phase 2

Phase 3

Phase 4

The work obviously has the same general structure as the previous example: ||:a:||:b + a':||. The melodic and harmonic means used to generate this structure, although more complex, are fundamentally only expansions of the kinds of things we heard operating in the trio of *Symphony 97*. Notice that the repeat of the *a* section is, as in that trio, varied in instrumentation, but in the minuet the variation is both more noticeable and more complex. Notice also the harmonic movement in relation to the phrase structure.

Listen to the *a* section alone (Example 9.7). As in the *a* section of the trio, here also there are two balanced phrases, the first moving from the tonic to the dominant (half cadence) and the second moving from the dominant back to the tonic (full cadence). Like the earlier example, too, the second phrase has a faster harmonic rhythm than the first. In addition the harmony in the second phrase is enriched by the use of chords other than I and V. Listen to the *a* section once more (Example 9.8) noting particularly the differences between the first and second phrases. The changes of harmony are indicated in Diagram 3.

**Diagram 3**

Listen now to the *b* section of the minuet (Example 9.9). As in the trio of *Symphony 97,* the balanced phrase structure of section *a* is no longer present in *b*, but unlike that of the trio, the *b* section here is longer than *a*. We hear fragments treated sequentially, there is a more active texture (two rhythmically independent lines), and later in *b* the motive from *a* is shortened so as to create a momentary shift in meter.

In *b*, then, a fragment of the theme becomes a building block; this process contrasts with the regular, balanced phrases of *a*. As a result *b* is more continuous. For example, there is a continuously directed motion to the twelfth measure of Section *b*, in contrast to the cadences which occur every four measures in Section *a*.

Consider now this first portion of *b* more closely, trying to discover what means Haydn uses to generate continuousness, tension, and contrast, through the development of material heard previously in *a*. There are three phases in the motion to the cadence in the twelfth measure of *b*, and a fourth phase which extends this cadence. What are the differences in affect and in the means used in these four phases (Example 9.10)?

The first phase has a wandering effect—we momentarily lose our bearings, we are in flux (*b*, measures 17–20). Following this, we sense, in Phase 2, a more directed tension (*b*, measures 21–24), and in Phase 3 the resolution of this tension in a cadence (*b*, measures 25–28). Finally, in Phase 4, we hear a kind of stasis (*b*, measures 29–35).

The harmonic means contributing to these changing effects are: in Phase 1, shifting tonality (a mixed family of pitches); in Phase 2, the establishment of the new key, first by an emphasis on its dominant—a waiting passage; and then, in Phase 3, through a cadential passage which has as its goal the solid arrival at the tonic, a full cadence in the new key. In Phase 4 the new tonic is extended by its reiteration in the bass with chord changes over it, some of them disturbing the stability of the new key. In addition, the stability of Phase 4 is weakened by an active texture and rhythmic conflict. Notice, for example, that the opening motive of *a* appears in truncated form in both the upper and lower parts of the texture in imitation. This results in a shift to duple meter, which conflicts with the prevailing triple meter and also sets up a cross-accent as the two fragments oppose one another. Following Diagram 4 now, listen to this part of Section *b* once more (Example 9.11). Comparisons among the four phases are summarized in Table 2.

**Diagram 4**

| Phase 1 | Phase 2 | Phase 3 | Phase 4 |
|---------|---------|---------|---------|
| Shifting tonality | V becomes tonic (waiting) | V–I in new key | Extension of new tonic |

**TABLE 2**

|  | 1 | 2–3 | 4 |
|---|---|---|---|
| *Affect:* | Instability, flux | Directed tension; then release | Stability (shaky) |
| *Means:* | Shifting tonality | Extended V of new key; then resolution to I of new key | Pedal on new tonic with chord changes above it |
| *Structural function:* | Modulation to the key of the dominant; tonic (G) → dominant (D) | Arrival at contrasting key area (D) | Confirmation of contrasting key area |

Thus, this passage creates a motion from the tonic (I) in the *a* section to the dominant (V) in the *b* section on the larger level of tonal centers themselves. In the *a* section a single tonal center was established through the movement of chords within that one key: I to V and back to I. Now, on a larger scale, and over a longer period of time, a harmonic motion has been generated from a key which we called the tonic to another key which we had previously heard as a dominant. In *a* we spoke of being *on* the dominant chord (at the end of Phrase 1) in *b* this same chord has become a tonic, and we speak of being *in* the dominant key. The process of moving from one key to another is called *modulation*.

We have hinted, however, that in Phase 4 the new key is not quite solidly established, there is still a certain restlessness—both in rhythm and in key. (Are we *on* the dominant or *in* the dominant?) In any case the dominant (key or chord) must resolve to the original tonic. Indeed, the return could take place at this point. Listen to how the *b* section would sound if *a* did return after Phase 4 of the *b* section (Example 9.12). Then listen to what Haydn actually does (Example 9.13). What is the difference?

In our artificial return the structural rhythm is speeded up; *b* is shortened and is not allowed to unwind itself gradually. Haydn, in contrast, slips back into *a* through a highly chromatic, unstable passage which even at its end generates a rather fuzzy "waiting passage." Thus Haydn has composed a kind of musical joke by preparing us for a return at the end of Phase 4 of *b* and then diverting this expectation with the sliding, modulatory, delaying passage which eases back to the tonic key and to the return of the thematic statement of *a*. Our feelings about the return, itself, are also different in Examples 9.12 and 9.13. The abrupt juxtaposition of *b* and *a* in Example 9.12 simply puts us down into the stability of *a*'s statement; in Example 9.13 the clarity and stability of key, phrase structure, texture, and rhythm in a' constitute not only a return to familiar material but a return to the comfort of stability after a period of feeling "Where am I? Where am I going?" In short, Haydn provides us with a more dramatic contrast than exists when the last phase of b is removed.

Listen now to the whole minuet (Example 9.14). You will notice that a returns with still further changes in instrumentation and with the addition of a coda. Comparing it with the trio from the Symphony 97, you will notice that the minuet has a considerably more dramatic effect. While the b section of the trio remained fixed harmonically and only hinted at a contrast in key area, this minuet, in its considerably lengthened b section, introduces modulation into a new key, establishes it (although we have some doubts in retrospect), and then wends its way back to the original key. Thus, the minuet is more dramatic because as you become aware of its details you respond to its greater variety of emotions over a longer period, although this variety is still on a small scale.

Harmonic Motion:
Stability and Instability
(side 11)

In this demonstration we are concerned with some further aspects of the complex subject of harmony. (Harmony, as a subject, occupies at least two years in a music student's course of study.) We will deal here with harmonic stability and instability, examining the following areas:

1. *Tonal stasis,* created by extended tonic harmony.
2. *Directed tension,* created by prolonged dominant harmony within one key (a *waiting passage*).
3. *Change of key,* either through the juxtaposition of two tonally stable areas each in a different key, or through the gradual change from one tonally stable area to another (modulation).
4. *Tonal ambiguity,* in contrast to directed tension, the tension created by an ambiguous or shifting tonality.

I

| Example | Composer, Title | Date |
|---------|-----------------|------|
| 10.1 | Schoenberg, *Gurrelieder* | 1901 |
| 10.2 | Beethoven, *Symphony 3,* fourth movement, ending | 1803 |

Examples 10.1 and 10.2 illustrate tonal stasis created by extended tonic harmony—seasoned with subdominant in Example 10.1. More static than stable (compared with the stability of a thematic statement), harmonic stasis functions differently in each of these two pieces. In Example 10.1 it serves as the prelude to a dramatic work and sets the scene

and mood; in Example 10.2 it brings an intense, rhythmically active movement to a conclusion— its braking motion providing a much-needed deceleration.

II

| Example | Composer, Title | Date |
|---------|-----------------|------|
| 10.3 | Rossini, *La Gazza Ladra,* overture | 1817 |
| 10.4 | Beethoven, *Egmont,* overture | 1809–1810 |
| 10.5 | Beethoven, *Symphony 8,* first movement | 1811 |
| 10.6 | Verdi, *Otello,* Act IV, scene 2 | 1887 |
| 10.7 | Schubert, *Quintet in C,* second movement | 1828 |

Examples 10.3 through 10.7 illustrate various kinds of directed tension. Examples 10.3 and 10.4 are waiting passages created by a dominant *pedal* (sustained or repeated tone). Where do these passages lead?

In Example 10.5 tension is directed to a return. Through manipulation and compression of the motive and the use of a crescendo, in conjunction with a series of chords harmonically surrounding the dominant out of which a clear dominant pedal finally emerges, the return is made overwhelming.

Example 10.6 illustrates a pedal (first played by the violins and then sung) in the upper part of the texture. The sustained tone occupies a variety of positions within the chromatically shifting chords; yet overall, almost in retrospect, it serves a dominant function. Thus this aria introduction functions as a kind of waiting passage.

Vaguely similar in harmonic function to the Verdi

excerpt, the Schubert quintet (Example 10.7) is nevertheless quite different in its scope and unrelenting intensity. Here the harmony creates an effect of endless search in which one loses all sense of time. The harmony is at times wandering (undirected), but it repeatedly approaches a cadence (directed tension), only to go on without reaching resolution. Finally the process is halted, not by arrival but by the appearance of a new element which is equally unstable. We have the feeling of being lost within a world of unending motion, searching for rest.

## III

| Example | Composer, Title | Date |
|---------|-----------------|------|
| 10.8 | Gould, *Spirituals* | 1941 |
| 10.9 | Mahler, *Symphony 1*, second movement | 1888 |
| 10.10 | Haydn, *Symphony 97*, first movement | 1792 |
| 10.11 | Beethoven, *Symphony 8*, first movement | 1812 |

Change of key provides a source of variety in harmonic color. In Examples 10.8 and 10.9 the change is immediate—that is, you hear the statement of a tune or motive in one key, then immediately begin again, either with the same material or with new material, but in a new key. There is no transition, only juxtaposition.

In contrast to these two examples, Examples 10.10 and 10.11 illustrate change of key by means of *modulation*, the gradual movement away from one tonal area (key) toward another, the process creating a momentary tonal "no-man's land." Notice that in the Haydn excerpt (Example 10.10) we leave one melody and arrive at the new key without another, while in the Beethoven example (Example 10.11) we arrive at both a new key and a new harmonically stable tune.

## IV

| Example | Composer, Title | Date |
|---------|-----------------|------|
| 10.12 | Haydn, *The Creation,* introduction ("Chaos") | 1798 |
| 10.13 | Liszt, *Faust Symphony,* beginning | 1854 |
| 10.14 | Beethoven, *String Quartet* (*Grosse Fuge*), Opus 133 | 1825 |
| 10.15 | Mozart, *String Quartet in D Minor,* K. 421, first movement | 1783 |

Finally, this section gives several examples of tonal ambiguity, examples in which the tonal "no-man's land," described above in relation to modulation, becomes almost the norm. Through continuous harmonic motion, which avoids any clear tonic or tonal direction, a strong sense of instability is created.

Examples 10.12 and 10.13 both occur at the beginning of a work, yet both are extremely unstable. In Example 10.12, by Haydn, one is constantly led to expect a different tonic cadence, but none ever comes. In the excerpt by Liszt (Example 10.13), expectation of a tonal center is hardly generated at all. The piece is extremely chromatic—that is, it is continuously moving and shifting its tonal framework—and the rate of change of events appears extremely slow.

Example 10.14, by Beethoven, sounds nearly

chaotic on first hearing. (Haydn's "chaos" is almost sublime order by comparison.) Harmonically the excerpt is an example of extreme chromaticism: at some moments we hear a series of shifting tonal centers, but at others tonality seems to be nearly obliterated. Listen to the example several times. Does it become less chaotic? What constitutes its means of achieving comprehensibility?

Listen now to Examples 10.2, 10.5, 10.11, and 10.14—one from each of the above groups—and you will hear one composer, Beethoven, using harmony like a palpable material for very different purposes and effects.

In Example 10.15 you hear a passage which seems at first unsure in its stability, then directed in its tension; this momentarily resolves only to veer away and continue on into tonal ambiguity generated by chromaticism coupled with intense dissonance. Next there is a sequential modulation under a more lyrical motive; this finally gives way to a directed waiting passage in preparation for the return to stability, both melodic and harmonic.

This "trip" encompasses all the varieties of harmonic effect discussed separately above, now operating dramatically within a single work: tonal ambiguity, modulation, an extended dominant pedal which clarifies the tonal direction, and finally, tonal stability—not the stasis of an extended tonic pedal but the stability of simple (I–IV–V) harmony which establishes a key.

The passage consists of the development section, preparation for return, and return in this quartet movement. Together with melodic fragmentation, an active texture, a large range, and the contrast of highly disjunct melodic motion with more conjunct motion, harmony is responsible for the changes in function and affect; that is, the progression from unstable development, to waiting, to thematic statement.

Harmony

*Paganini*
Eugene Delacroix, c. 1830
(The Phillips Collection, Washington)

# FORM
# AND FUNCTION 7

## SECTIONAL
## ORGANIZATION

In this chapter we come finally to the consideration
of whole works, where we bring together the various aspects of music which have, of necessity,
been discussed separately throughout the book.
We are at a point which might be described as the
"denouement"—the moment when, as forecast in
the Introduction, you should be able to perceive
the effects of the various aspects of music "not as
isolated factors but as parts of an inseparable
whole, combining and influencing one another to
generate the events, motion, and process of a
unique work." In this section we will be concerned
with specific musical forms as such, observing
particularly the varying roles or functions of certain
passages within the context of these forms.

Please note that in dealing with *sectional* forms—
specifically, the minuet and sonata form—we will
concentrate on music written after the middle of
the eighteenth century. Sectional forms became
more prevalent after 1750 due to a number of
stylistic factors, the most significant of which was
the emergence of tonality as a fundamental syntactical force. Our purpose here is not to give a

survey of sectional forms (by including all types from all periods), but rather to consider carefully the general characteristics of two forms and through these considerations to refine further your musical perception.

It is important to make a distinction between the immediate experience of a work and those abstract concepts called musical forms which represent a generalization from many works that share, in some sense, the same structure (such as the minuet, sonata form, and rondo). On the one hand, the direct experience of a work is that of a series of events—we are speaking, now, of events on a larger scale—which we grasp, at first, in terms of passages of stability, moving away, tension, agitation, culmination, and so forth; and then later in terms of structural function, such as statement of a theme, digression, development, return, or ending. This series of events, when completed, constitutes the form; and, depending on their inner relationships, we can go from the particular experience of these events to a more generalized experience, recognizing the totality as a minuet, a sonata form, a rondo, a theme and variations, or some other structure.

On the other hand, we can begin, as we do in Demonstration 11, with the abstract concept of a form, in which case we anticipate the order of events, perceiving the *distinctions* among a number of works all of which share, in the most general sense, the same organizing principle. We can then watch with fascination (as we did in choosing the examples) as each piece unfolds some of the myriad possibilities that composers have found for realizing a single, basically simple structure—differences stemming from the predilections of the composer at the moment, as well as from changes in musical style. (The examples in Demonstration 11 span a period of 138 years.) The informed but inexperienced listener will probably feel more comfortable with the second approach; the informed and experienced listener will take both approaches simultaneously, responding to the unique events of each piece as they happen, but also enjoying the process as a particular experience within a more general framework.

| Example | Composer, Title | Date |
|---------|-----------------|------|
| 11.1 | Mozart, *German Dance*, K. 605, no. 1 | 1791 |
| 11.2 | Haydn, *Symphony 99*, minuet | 1793 |
| 11.3 | Mozart, *Symphony 40*, minuet | 1788 |
| 11.4 | Beethoven, *Quartet*, Opus 18, no. 1, scherzo | 1799 |
| 11.5 | Schubert, *Quintet in C*, scherzo (without trio and scherzo *da capo* | 1828 |
| 11.6 | Mendelssohn, *Symphony 4*, third movement | 1833 |
| 11.7 | Mahler, *Symphony 1*, second movement | 1888 |
| 11.8 | Schoenberg, *Suite for Piano*, Opus 25, minuet | 1925 |

On the most general level the pieces in Demonstration 11 (all of which are in triple meter) can be described as shown in Diagram 1. In a few ex-

**Diagram 1**

| A | B | A' |
|---|---|---|
| minuet | trio | minuet (*da capo*)[1] |
| ‖:a:‖:b + a':‖ | ‖:c:‖:d + c':‖ | a b + a' |

amples the trio and minuet *da capo* have not been included, due to lack of time-space. The sections are indicated on the record, although not exactly at the beginning of the sections, so that you may experience these structural events yourself.

[1]*Da capo* (D.C.) is an indication to the performers to go back to the beginning and play the first part of the piece over again. It is most often found at the end of the trio section, indicating a replaying of the minuet ("minuet *da capo*").

Structure: Process
and Design

150

Each composer has played with the possibilities inherent in this general schema. Notice particularly the following:

1. The nature of the return to a'. Is there a "waiting passage" or not? Is the return varied?
2. The development of thematic material. Where does it occur, or does it?
3. The nature of the contrast between a and b.
4. The nature of the contrast between the minuet (or A section) and the trio.
5. The addition or lack of a coda.
6. The proportions of the whole and the parts to the whole.
7. The nature of the thematic material itself, and how it influences the realization of the overall structure.

As you listen to this collection of works you should discover a richer significance in the simple notion of statement–contrast–return (set forth in Exercise 2 and Demonstration 7) and the influence that stylistic change can have on it.

Example 11.1, Mozart's *German Dance,* presents the structure in its irreducible form; in Example 11.2, from Haydn's *Symphony 99,* the proportions of the movement are expanded. You will remember that in studying this piece previously (Chapter 5, Additional Materials), we noted that a, itself, included three sections, each with a different function: a statement (consisting of antecedent and consequent phrases), an extension and elaboration of this material, and a closing section. Contrast in b is created by developmental treatment of the initial thematic material—inversion, fragmentation, a more active texture, and harmonic instability. The return is prepared by the gradual emergence of the opening material. We move from an imitative statement of the initial motive into a complete statement of the original theme with its clear, homo-

**MINUET**

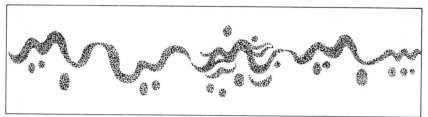

**TRIO**

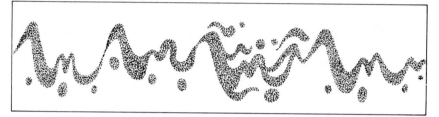

**MINUET *DA CAPO***

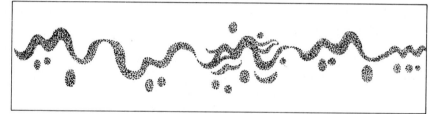

phonic texture. Notice that the change in a' creates a sense of greater finality—that is, what was in a an elaboration or exploration of implications, becomes in a' their resolution. The trio contrasts with the minuet in its more lyrical character, softer dynamics, reduced orchestral forces, and the smaller dimensions of its structure. The trio follows the same general structure as the minuet, but a brief transition section is added before the return to the minuet in order to effect the modulation from the distant key of the trio to the original key of the movement.

Structure: Process
and Design

152

The most unusual aspect of the form in Example 11.3, from Mozart's Symphony 40, is the nature of a', which you may have difficulty hearing as a return. Mozart presumes a great familiarity with the norm—he prepares the return at the end of b and, in fact, does return to the original key, but the return is so polyphonic that the melody derived from a is swallowed up in the intensely active texture. Rather than a restored sense of stability, the effect is of an intensification of the development found in b, clarification coming only in the woodwind coda, which is more like a *codetta* ("little coda"). Note also in listening to this movement the many ways in which the trio contrasts with the minuet.

The third movement of a symphony or quartet changes in Beethoven's hands from a minuet to a scherzo; while the "form" remains, the character of the scherzo removes it even further than the two previous movements from its elegant courtly origins. Notice the following in Example 11.4 (from Beethoven's *Quartet*, Opus 18, no. 1):

1. The extreme brevity of a and, to a lesser degree, of b.
2. The great expansion that takes place in a'.
3. In the trio, the almost unrecognizable return of c'.
4. The lack of repetition of d + c', which stems from the varied nature of c'.

What does the nature of the thematic material itself do to the return? At what point in the process do we finally feel the stability usually associated with return?

Example 11.5, taken from Schubert's *Quintet in C,* is the longest of all the movements heard thus far. Unlike in Example 11.4 the a section of this scherzo is expanded also, making a work in which all the

Form
and Function

153

sections (*a*, *b*, and *a'*) are nearly equal in length. Notice that the opening material is already considerably elaborated in *a*: the harmony becomes more complex, contrasting material is introduced, and the section ends with a codetta. The *b* section introduces not only further development of the opening material of *a*, but also a new melody (though one that seems to derive from *a* material). The *b* section leads into *a'* with a prolonged waiting passage (this passage was included in Demonstration 5 as Example 5.15, showing a complex rhythmic structure which "clears up" at the return). At the end of *a'* a coda is added. In this performance *b* + *a'* is not repeated.

While the music you have heard thus far in this demonstration spans a period of only 40 years (1788–1828), its departures from the norm are remarkable. The changes can perhaps best be summarized by noting the relative proportions of stable melodic statements to unstable elaborations, developments, and codas. While the *German Dance* is primarily composed of melodies—their appearance, disappearance into brief "development," and reappearance—the later works are primarily occupied with realizing the *implications* of briefly stated thematic material—material which is, itself, often dramatic and unstable. As a result, the character and purpose of the minuet is transformed dramatically from its original function as music for the royal ballroom.

Example 11.6, from Mendelssohn's *Symphony 4*, is more lyrical in character than any of the previous examples. Unlike them it is entitled neither "minuet" nor "scherzo," but simply marked *con moto* (literally, "with motion," "quick")—an indication of tempo, to some degree, and also of the character of the piece and the attitude to be taken in its performance. Once again the movement follows the same general structure as the other movements designated "minuet" or "scherzo," and it also occupies the usual third-movement position in the symphony as a whole. Only the A section is included, the trio and *da capo* being omitted. Notice that the *a'* section is quite varied, so that it sounds more final than the original *a*. The lack of repeat of *b* + *a'* is consistent with the conclusiveness of the varied return.

The movement by Mahler from *Symphony 1* (Example 11.7, marked simply *Kräftig bewegt*—"lively, animated") derives from two seemingly disparate musical phenomena: the simple, diatonic tunes of the Austrian village band, and a very large orchestra and much expanded (chromatic) harmonic vocabulary. The result is a piece rich in contrasts in sonority and full of "sound effects." In relation to the structure of A, notice the following: (1) there are no repeats; (2) *b* is relatively long in relation to *a* and has greater contrast in sonority and texture; note particularly the increase in textural activity and the thickening of the texture at the climax, followed by a thinning of the texture down to only one group of instruments at the waiting passage before the return of *a'*; and (3) that *a'* is introduced softly and with a thin texture followed by a full orchestration of the original theme, which is then varied to create a dramatic coda. The trio provides contrast in almost every dimension and is freely structured. The return to A includes essentially only the *a'* section with its coda.

In Example 11.8 from his *Suite for Piano,* Opus 25, Schoenberg has adapted the old minuet form to a new harmonic context—chromatic and without a tonal center. What creates stability of thematic

Form
and Function

155

statement and instability of development? The traditional structure within the minuet is, in many senses, maintained: a is repeated literally; b + a', however, is not (literal repeats are rare in Schoenberg); and only portions of a return exactly in a'. The larger structure—minuet–trio–minuet da capo —is also maintained.

It is interesting to note that the sense of dramatic possibility which we saw emerging even in the earlier minuets is further emphasized in Examples 11.6 to 11.8. In particular the returns are consistently more varied, generating within the structure exactly the kind of drama—almost in the narrative sense—that is inherent in the attitude which sought a new kind of personal expression in the Romantic Period.

# Demonstration 12
## Sonata Form
### (side 13)

This demonstration differs from Demonstration 11 in two ways: (1) While in Demonstration 11 we began with an abstract concept, minuet form, in Demonstration 12 we begin with the events themselves, concentrating on the varying functions which passages can assume, only later arriving at the generalization, the concept—in this case, *sonata form.* (2) In Demonstration 11 we considered a number of examples written over a relatively long time span and reflecting great diversity in musical style; in Demonstration 12 we concentrate on the music of only two composers, Mozart and Beethoven, and all the examples were written within a period of about 40 years. In addition, we consider only one work in its entirety.

The difference in approach between these two demonstrations stems largely from the nature of the sonata form itself, particularly its greater length and complexity. Because the form demands from

| Example | Composer, Title | Date |
|---------|-----------------|------|
| 12.1 | Mozart, *Symphony 40,* K. 550, fourth movement, measures 125–205 | 1788 |
| 12.2 | measures 1–32 | |
| 12.3 | Beethoven, *Symphony 9,* first movement, measures 1–29 | 1823 |
| 12.4 | Beethoven, *Quartet,* Opus 18, no. 1, first movement, measures 101–114 | 1799 |
| 12.5 | measures 101–154 | |
| 12.6 | measures 115–186 | |
| 12.7 | Mozart, *Quartet in G Major,* K. 387, first movement | 1782 |

the listener greater concentration and involvement over a longer period of time, a more thorough experience within a single style would seem more productive. (In the Additional Materials section, examples of movements in sonata form from later periods are suggested.)

Compare Examples 12.1 and 12.2; listen to them several times. While they both work with the same material, one of the passages is more stable. Why? Which of the two might be the opening statement of the theme? Example 12.2 is the initial *statement* of the theme; Example 12.1 is a subsequent *development* of it. The initial statement, with its regular, stable harmonic movement (emphasis on tonic and dominant chords) has the clear (and by now familiar) structure shown in Diagram 1.

**Diagram 1**

‖:   *a*   :‖:   *b + a'*   :‖

8         8
measures measures

Listen to Example 12.2 once again.

Later in the movement Mozart develops this theme, beginning rather as he does originally, but quickly breaking it up, dissecting it, and in effect keeping the listener guessing by avoiding clear tonality, rhythm, and phrasing. Listen to Example 12.1 again.

We hear in Examples 12.1 and 12.2 the kind of harmonic contrast (tonal stability and instability) discussed in Demonstration 10, but now operating within one work in passages in which the composer uses basically the same motivic material. These two excerpts illustrate a basic distinction in the presentation of musical materials; we might describe them as music of *being*, that is, thematic

Structure: Process
and Design

158

statement; and music of *becoming,* that is, developmental or transitional material. But music of *becoming* can take other forms. Consider Example 12.3 by Beethoven. Here we listen with fascination as something grows out of almost nothing. We hear how the theme, stated by the full orchestra almost in unison, has its origin in the two-note figure heard at the very beginning, and how the mystery and tentativeness of the opening yield to the forthright, open thematic statement. We move from music of *becoming* to music of *being.*

Next listen to Example 12.4 to determine its character and where you think it falls in the movement. It is a *closing section.* Almost opposite in effect to the previous example, this excerpt closes off a large section of a work. The static harmony restrains the forceful rhythmic and melodic motives. Over an embellished tonic pedal played by the cello, the other instruments play, with rhythmic regularity, a series of V–I progressions followed by scale passages which have the effect of further extending or elaborating the tonic harmony.

Listen to it again with its continuation (Example 12.5). In marked contrast to the closing section, this continuation is highly unstable, charged with excitement—modulating, avoiding clear cadences, and in general being characterized by a rapid rate of change. The passage is concerned with *development,* or analysis in the sense of the breaking-up of previously stated material. This continuation constitutes the first half of the *development section* of the movement.

Now listen to the entire development section and its continuation (Example 12.6). Here we have an exciting experience of return to familiar territory, to stable ground, in fact to the tonic of the piece and to the very opening of the work. This return

Form
and Function

159

is anticipated by a lengthy *waiting passage,* an ornamented dominant pedal with a very agitated rhythm (heard previously as D5.25).

Finally, Example 12.7 presents the entire first movement of Mozart's *Quartet in G Major,* K. 387. It falls into nine sections more or less clearly articulated by the kinds of contrasts we have heard in previous examples, but now operating within one movement. Each section has its role, its *function,* in the evolution of the total work. Listen carefully and differentiate among the functions of these sections. Ask yourself the following questions:

1. Is there a tune or a well-defined *thematic statement,* with clear phrasing and stable harmony?
2. Or is the music unstable, fragmented, changing frequently in texture, and harmonically ambiguous or modulating—thus *transitional* or *developmental* in character?
3. Or is the harmonic movement directed to a certain goal—a *waiting passage?*
4. Or does the music seem to be cadential in some way—a *closing section?*

Listen to the entire movement at least once before reading the analysis of it which follows. It is in what is called *sonata form* and consists of the following sections:

Section 1 states the opening theme, material from which is used prominently throughout the entire movement. The phrasing is clear, the harmony stable within the key of the tonic, G Major.

In Section 2 the thematic material is fragmented; there is a change to a more active texture, contrast in textural density, and imitation. The passage is much more continuous and is modulatory in harmony, finally arriving at a waiting passage in the

Structure: Process
and Design

160

key of the dominant in preparation for the statement of another theme—in sum, this is a *transition section.*

Section 3 presents a contrasting tune. (What gives it a character different from that of the opening theme?) Its phrase structure is less balanced, but clear, and its harmony is stable.

Section 4 is a *closing section,* a series of extended cadences always returning, sometimes with delay, to the tonic of the section.

Sections 1–4 together constitute the **exposition** of the movement.

Section 5, a **development** section, is characterized by the greatest rate of change; motives from the themes of the exposition are manipulated and thrown off balance. We are ushered into the development with a marvelously unsettling distortion of the opening theme. As it proceeds, the tone colors of the instruments are exploited and the texture varies in both activity and density. The harmony is at first ambiguous, then shifts from one key to another, coming to rest with a passage reminiscent of the closing section of the exposition. But the deceptiveness of this closing is revealed as we move into a waiting passage which prepares the return of the opening theme. Once more we find ourselves back on stable ground.

Sections 6–9 together constitute the **recapitulation**; they parallel Sections 1–4 of the exposition. Thus in Section 6 we have the opening theme; Section 7 parallels Section 2 (the transition); Section 8 parallels Section 3, stating the second, contrasting theme. Finally, Section 9 parallels Section 4, the closing section which completes the movement. Listen again to the entire movement. Its dramatic

Form
and Function

evolution is generated by the composer's genius and skill, his command over those musical means previously discussed and now heard operating in guises appropriate to making this movement a whole: sonority and texture, rhythmic and melodic shapes contrasting and combining, and varieties of harmonic motion.

**EXPOSITION**

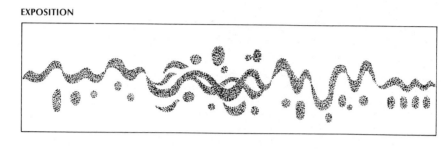

**DEVELOPMENT**

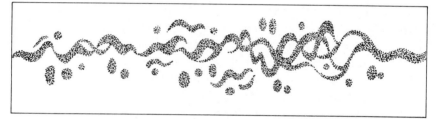

**RECAPITULATION**

The generalized structure of the Mozart quartet movement, or of any movement in sonata form, can be outlined as follows.

Structure: Process
and Design

# SONATA FORM

**(Introduction.)** Slow, exploratory, and wandering in character; modulatory and often tonally ambiguous until just before the end; leads directly into the exposition.

## Exposition.

1. *Theme Group 1.* One or more themes in the tonic key, characterized by the harmonic stability and generally regular phrasing of thematic statement.
2. *Transition.* Modulating, generally more active in texture, athematic, more continuous.
3. *Theme Group 2.* One or more themes in another key (usually the dominant) which contrast in character with those of Theme Group 1.
4. *Closing Section.* Cadential in effect; closes off the exposition with emphasis on the new tonic.

## Development.

5. "Analysis" and exploration of material presented in the exposition, characterized by modulation, tonal ambiguity, melodic fragmentation, and rapid rate of change. This section is more active in texture and more continuous; occasionally a new theme is presented.

**Recapitulation.** A repetition of the sequence of the exposition:

6. *Theme Group 1.*
7. *Transition.*
8. *Theme Group 2.* Now in the tonic of the piece.
9. *Closing Section.*

**(Coda.)** May take the form of further development of material before ending the piece in an even more final fashion than the closing section.

Two points should be made about the above outline as a generalization—and these are opposite in their emphasis:

1.  The sonata form (or any musical form) as described in a diagram is a generalization made from a large number of works, each of which is unique—as you have seen in listening to the minuets. That is, form does not mean a mold like those into which you pour gelatin, hoping that each salad will be identical. The generalization is most useful, in fact, not in categorizing or labeling but in perceiving distinctions. Given sufficient time and experience, you can come to hear within the framework of a given form not devices or formal sections but rather organic movement, function— you can respond to the composer's musical gestures.

2.  Our second point concerns the effect your knowledge of forms has on your expectations. For example, when you listen to the first movement of a symphony by Mozart you can with justification anticipate a different series of events from those that will occur when you listen to the third movement, since the first movement will almost certainly be in sonata form, while the third will be a minuet.

What are the differences in your expectations for these two movements? The first-movement sonata form is larger in every sense. More happens. There are two contrasting statement areas; these require a transition between them and often a closing section before the development. The development is the heart of the sonata concept; here the composer reveals to the listener the implications of what may have seemed straightforward, simple melodies in the exposition. The recapitulation, in turn, is not heard as simply a repeat of the exposition—you hear the music now in a new light, having experienced the development where the potentialities of the thematic material were explored. Thus this first-movement form, as it is sometimes called (though not correctly, since it may occur in a second or final movement), is expansive, organic, and dramatic. So much happens in a movement in sonata form—transformations in character, conflict, revelations of hidden implications, and so forth.

In the minuet your expectations are different. The experience is of two usually quite separate wholes and a third which repeats the first; that is, minuet–trio–minuet. This is quite different from the experience of dramatic growth in the sonata form. Considering any of the three parts of the minuet (since we do consider them separately), our sense of proportions is much smaller than it is when we hear the sonata form. There is but one theme presented in the *a* section; development of the material of *a*, primarily in the *b* section, is on a considerably smaller scale than what we can expect in the development section of a sonata form movement; and return will be less dramatic because of the shorter, less revealing excursion.

Put in these terms, however, the comparison is inherently dangerous, since it pits the minuet against the sonata. Our point is that each must be heard in its own terms. We must listen to the way each composer realizes or exploits the possibilities of a particular set of formal relationships. Thus, on the one hand each piece must be heard as a unique series of events; but at the same time these events must be perceived as realizing, in some way, that set of formal relationships which the piece shares with other works.

Form
and Function

## Exercise 5
## Structural Functions
## (side 14)

Following the discussion in Demonstration 12 of the different functions of passages within a sonata form movement, this exercise offers you the opportunity to "test" your ability to perceive these musical events. As in the demonstration, we have chosen excerpts from instrumental works by Mozart and Beethoven. These two composers, along with Haydn, are the "great men" of the Classical Period (c. 1750 to 1827; 1827 being the year of Beethoven's death), the period in which the sonata form became a fundamental way of thinking for composers of instrumental music.

| Example | A | B | C | D |
|---------|---|---|---|---|
| 5.1 | | | | |
| 5.2 | | | | |
| 5.3 | | | | |
| 5.4 | | | | |
| 5.5 | | | | |
| 5.6 | | | | |
| 5.7 | | | | |
| 5.8 | | | | |
| 5.9 | | | | |
| 5.10 | | | | |
| 5.11 | | | | |
| 5.12 | | | | |
| 5.13 | | | | |

Structure: Process
and Design

Listen to each passage twice; determine whether it may be characterized as:

A. Statement.
B. Transitional-development.
C. Waiting passage.
D. Closing passage.

Then check the corresponding column in the table on the facing page. Answers are given on page 168.

²Examples of waiting passages include brief statements of the thematic material into which they lead.

*Correct*
*Answers*

| Example | Composer, Title | A | B | C | D |
|---------|-----------------|---|---|---|---|
| 5.1 | Beethoven, *Quartet,* Opus 18, no. 1, first movement, 1799 | X | | | |
| 5.2 | Beethoven, *Quartet,* Opus 18, no. 1, second movement, 1799 | | | | X |
| 5.3 | Beethoven, *Sonata for Violin,* Opus 30, no. 2, third movement, 1802 | | | X | |
| 5.4 | Beethoven, *Quartet,* Opus 18, no. 1, fourth movement, 1799 | X | | | |
| 5.5 | Mozart, *Symphony 40,* K. 550, first movement, 1788 | X | | | |
| 5.6 | Mozart, *Symphony 40,* K. 550, first movement, 1788 | | X | | |
| 5.7 | Beethoven, *Quartet,* Opus 18, no. 1, fourth movement, 1799 | | X | | |
| 5.8 | Beethoven, *Quartet,* Opus 18, no. 1, fourth movement, 1799 | | | X | |
| 5.9 | Beethoven, *Quartet,* Opus 18, no. 4, first movement, 1799 | X | | | |
| 5.10 | Beethoven, *Quartet,* Opus 18, no. 4, first movement, 1799 | | X | | |
| 5.11 | Beethoven, *Symphony 4,* first movement, 1806 | | | X | |
| 5.12 | Beethoven, *Symphony 4,* first movement, 1806 | | | | X |
| 5.13 | Mozart, *Quartet in G,* K. 387, first movement, 1782 | | | | X |

Structure: Process
and Design

## CONTINUOUS ORGANIZATION

Demonstration 13

Prelude and Fugue

(side 14)

In Demonstration 7, "Sectional and Continuous Organization," we discussed two fundamentally different approaches to musical design. In Demonstrations 11 and 12 we dealt with only one of these—sectional organization—concentrating particularly on works which, as a result of their clear sections, can be described in terms of specific musical forms. However, the discussion of sonata form should have made it clear that sectional structures may include areas which are continuous in effect; indeed, it is the contrast between the more clearly sectional passages (statements) and the more ongoing passages (development and transition) which contributes greatly to the variety and drama of sonata form.

It is important at this point to make clear that the kind of schematic representation appropriate to the minuet and, to some extent, to sonata form is applicable to hardly any other large body of music. For instance, listen to Example 13.1 (heard before as D7.2). It was pointed out in Demonstration 7 that despite the clear breaks in the flow of the Chopin prelude, it is fundamentally *continuous* and defies schematic representation. The "pauses" are never full cadences (on the tonic); they do not create stable points of arrival. The general harmonic instability coupled with the continuous outpouring of notes propels you forward without stop. The sense of the piece as a single, cumulative gesture results not only from its brevity but also from its

| Example | Composer, Title | Date |
|---------|-----------------|------|
| 13.1 | Chopin, *Prelude*, Opus 28, no. 18 | 1838 |
| 13.2 | Bach, *Well-Tempered Clavier*, Book I, Prelude no. 2 in C Minor | 1722 |
| 13.3 | Bach, *Well-Tempered Clavier*, Book I, Prelude and Fugue no. 3 in C-sharp Major | 1722 |
| 13.4 | fugue, measures 1 and 2 | |
| 13.5 | fugue, measures 1–7 | |
| 13.6 | fugue, measures 1–10 | |
| 13.7 | fugue, measures 1–12 | |
| 13.8 | fugue, measures 1–22 | |
| 13.9 | entire fugue | |

tight unity of motivic and harmonic material. Notice how each impulse grows motivically out of the previous one—expanding or compressing it—to generate an improvisatory, impetuous character by its flexibility of pulse and rhythm. It is interesting to note Chopin's final "statement"—two chords, V to I. Yet, because of the particular positioning of these last chords, the piece does not seem to come to a full stop. Consistent with its continuous flow, we listen on until the sound has died away.

Next compare the Chopin prelude with Prelude no. 2 in C Minor from Bach's *Well-Tempered Clavier* (Example 13.2, heard previously as E2.4). The Bach prelude differs from Chopin's in its steady pulse, homogeneous rhythmic motion, texture, and harmonic movement. But near the end there is, within this particular framework, a dramatic change: the texture becomes varied both in density and activity, the pulse is lost, the rhythm becomes freer, and the harmony no longer moves with regularity either in pace or in direction. The ending has an improvisatory air; but even the first part of the piece, with its unchanging rhythmic and harmonic motion and its avoidance of clearly defined full cadences, creates a sense of free elaboration defying any kind of schematic or formal representation.

Listen now to another prelude by Bach and the fugue which was written to follow it (Example 13.3, Prelude and Fugue no. 3 in C-sharp Major). Notice that this prelude is similar in character to the previous one—a continuous and basically homogeneous elaboration including subtle changes in texture. But unlike the C minor prelude, it does not pause and never loses the sense of a clear and regular pulse. As you listen to the fugue which follows consider where you would place it on a continuum that ranges from sectional organization at one extreme (for example, Mozart's German Dance, D7.1, D11.1) through works in which sectional and continuous moments are contrasted (such as sonata form movements), to, at the other extreme, continuous works like the preludes.

On first hearing, you would probably place the fugue near the continuous extreme due to its textural, rhythmic, and motivic homogeneity, and because it is not easily divisible into clearly articulated sections. But closer listening will reveal its various "phases," although each one merges with the next (no caesurae) through continuous melodic and rhythmic activity. Listen again to the opening of the fugue (Example 13.4)—a single melodic line— noticing particularly the lilting, almost catchy, character of the melody, created in part by the contrast between faster, conjunct motion leading to slower, highly disjunct motion. Compare this opening thematic statement with the opening statements of the sonata form movements discussed in Demonstration 12 and the Additional Materials section at the end of this chapter, particularly in terms of the developmental possibilities inherent in each.

This opening statement in a fugue is called the

Form
and Function

171

*subject,* and we quickly discover that the entire fugue is concerned with it. Indeed, the fugue can be thought of as a development and manipulation of the motives of its subject—a continuous exploration of its implications and possibilities.

This fugue continues with the entrance in "imitation" of the two other participants, the middle and lower voices, which complete the texture. (Fugues may have any number of participating voices but the usual number is three, four, or five.) Notice, as you listen to the next example (Example 13.5), that each voice enters with a complete statement of the subject. However, when the middle voice enters, the top voice continues with a related melody played "against" the subject, thus called the *countersubject.* As the third voice enters, the two higher voices continue; the texture grows progressively thicker and more complex. This portion of the fugue, which introduces all the participants, each stating the subject, is called the *exposition.* It may be diagrammed as shown in Diagram 1. Fugal expositions have been heard previously in D3.14, E1.9, E3.10, and E3.11.

**Diagram 1**

H:      subject      countersubject   free material _ _

          M:      subject      countersubject

                    L:      subject

To use the same word, "exposition," to describe both the opening phase of the fugue and the first large section of the sonata form seems hardly appropriate. And in fact, a comparison of these two expositions will reveal some of the striking differences between the two approaches to musical design. You may want to consider these differences after completing the discussion of the fugue.

Structure: Process
and Design

Listen once more to the exposition of this fugue and the following short continuation (Example 13.6). How does the continuation differ from the exposition?

The continuation, of course, does not include a statement of the subject; instead, rhythmic and melodic fragments of the subject and counter-subject are treated sequentially. These phases of the fugue, in which the subject does not appear in its entirety, are called *episodes*, the term suggesting their freer and more continuous character. What is important in our discussion is the effect of greater instability in the episodes: the parts are somewhat more equal in importance (in the sense that the subject does not predominate), the subject has lost its integrity, the key changes through sequential development, and often the relative regularity of structural rhythm is lost; that is, the normative rhythmic unit (the length of the subject) is disrupted. This contrast between phases in which the subject is present and those in which it is not is crucial to the inner motion of the fugue. As the subject becomes submerged in the intricacies of the episodes, we have a sense of instability and tension. The reappearance of the subject provides relative stability in the otherwise continuous flow.

Listen once more (Example 13.7) to the first part of the fugue to see if you can hear when the subject returns. The subject reappears in the top voice—emerging subtly out of the freely flowing material of the episode. Listen to Example 13.7 again and notice how the rhythmic and melodic shape of the subject—particularly its large leaps coinciding with regular, pulse-like accents—seems to take over and momentarily dominate the texture, giving the listener a more specific focus for his attention.

Once more we will begin with the exposition, but this time we will continue on to the quasi-caesura (*quasi* because one of the parts continues on), which occurs about one-third of the way through the fugue (Example 13.8). Listen for the contrast between subject statements and episodes and also for the differences among the statements of the subject and among the episodes. (Is the subject heard clearly, or is it hidden within the texture? Is it prepared for in some way—by a thinning of the texture or a decrease in the textural activity, for example—or do you become aware of its presence only after it has already begun?)

The fugue up to the quasi-caesura can be diagrammed as in Diagram 2.

Listen to Example 13.8 again, following the diagram.

Now listen to the whole fugue (Example 13.9). Notice that after the cadential episode (Episode 4), Bach plays with the "head" of the subject, teasing the listener by not completing the statement

**Diagram 2**

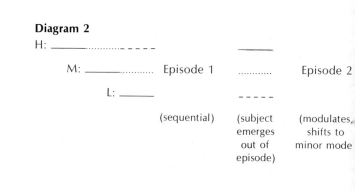

(Episode 5). After this short episode there are two more statements of the subject—one right after the other—followed by a long episode which uses both the beginning and ending motives from the subject. The last part of the episode functions as a waiting passage. This passage is harmonically static on the dominant, with an ornamented pedal first in the lowest and then in the highest voice. The opening fragment of the subject is heard in sequential repetition, producing in the listener an increasing desire for the complete statement. The subject finally appears clearly in the top voice; the texture thins (the lowest voice alone playing with the subject); and the key is that of the opening. This entrance is followed by statements in the middle and lower voices much like those we heard in the exposition. (Is this a return?) There follows an episode which remains in the tonic key, providing the harmonic stability of ending. Finally, one more statement of the subject is heard, ending on a deceptive cadence, followed by a cadential passage concluding with four chords reminiscent of the end of the subject as well as the conclusion of the preceding prelude.

- - - - -                    - - - - -

Episode 3        _____        Episode 4

_____           ............

(minor mode,    (sequential,    (subject        (cadential,
  texture         modulating)     rather          texture
  thins)                          submerged,      becomes
                                  minor mode)     less active,
                                                  chords in
                                                  lower parts,
                                                  return to
                                                  major)

The last part of the fugue can be illustrated as in Diagram 3.

**Diagram 3**

H: ———............                    ———...............– – – –              ———– – – –

Episode 5  M: – – – – ———  Episode 6       ——— ............  Episode 7  ..............– – – –

L: ..............– – – –              ..............– – – ———                – – – – – – – –

| (head of subject in sequence) | (subject sneaks in) | (extended sequence— ending with waiting passage) |

Listen to the fugue several times noting the contrasts between episodes and subject entries. Despite these contrasts, you will certainly hear the piece as an extremely homogeneous whole; one reason for this is that when the second voice and the countersubject have entered, all the material of the piece has been introduced. How different this procedure is from sonata form, with its clearly differentiated areas and dramatic contrasts! The listening process must also be different: to expect in a fugue the kind of contrast that one finds in a sonata form—contrasts in theme, character, texture, rate of events, and often instrumentation— will blind the listener to its pleasures. In listening to the fugue one becomes increasingly fascinated not only with the appearance and disappearance of the subject, but also with the subtle changes in texture and sonority, such as the relative degrees of motion in the various strands or the differences in sonority depending on which voice has the subject and what kind of activity surrounds it.

In a certain sense the fugue is player's rather than listener's music; the player, with the music before him, is extremely aware of the texture and its

Structure: Process
and Design

176

component lines. Yet in a work which may sound much the same all the way through, which is monothematic and might even be termed mono-chromatic, the listener comes to hear the subtle changes within its homogenous, continuous struc-ture, to perceive the art in the midst of artifice.

The music of this fugue is printed in the following pages. However well (or poorly) you read music, you will be interested in following the music as you listen to the entire fugue. The episodes and reentries of the subject and countersubject are indicated in the music. Sit down at your harpsi-chord and play!

**Fugue No. 3**
**in C-Sharp Major**

J. S. BACH

subject
countersubject

Episode 6

30

Waiting passage (dominant pedal = x)

40

Episode 7

50

Cadential

## ADDITIONAL
## MATERIALS

I

Mozart, *Symphony 40,* fourth movement, 1788
Haydn, *Symphony 97,* first movement, 1792
Beethoven, *Symphony 4,* first movement, 1806

These three works (many others are possible) are suggested as illustrations of large, symphonic sonata form movements. They exemplify some of the diverse possibilities found by these three composers, who wrote in a relatively similar style and within the same structural framework. Listen to each of them several times. First, on the immediate level of a series of events, consider the differences among them in overall character. Then, using the generalized model on p. 163, compare the three movements in terms of structure, proportions, and the musical means used to generate these structural relationships. Consider the following questions:

1.  Is there an introduction? How does it relate to the exposition? How would the piece sound without it?
2.  What are the differences in character of the opening themes, and what musical means are used to generate these differences? How are these differences related to the presence or absence of an introduction? Compare the differences in the proportions of these first theme statements.
3.  How does the transition emerge out of the statement? What thematic material does it use? Is it immediately evident that you have left the stable statement? When and how does the composer move away from the first theme and key? What is the nature of the arrival at the new theme—is it delayed (the transition prolonged)? Is there a waiting passage, a pause, or a gradual emergence of the

Structure: Process
and Design

new theme? What is the difference in proportions among the transition passages, especially in relation to the first theme group?

4. What is the nature of the contrast between the first and second theme groups in each piece? What means are used to generate this contrast (such as instrumentation, melodic-rhythmic shape, or harmony)? Are there similarities among the works?

5. What about the closing section? What proportion of the exposition does it occupy? Does it include a new (closing) theme? What means does each composer use to establish stability? Is the exposition repeated on your recording?

6. How does the development section begin? Are you aware at once that this is development—that is, is it immediately unstable, modulatory, or ambiguous in harmony? Do you hear manipulation and distortion of thematic material? What material from the exposition is developed in this section? Is new material introduced? What else does the composer do? Are there contrasts in texture and sonority? Is there a climax? Does the development fall into several sections? How does each composer "get back"? Through an extended waiting passage? Through the gradual emergence of stability and theme? At the climax or after it? What about the length of the development in relation to the exposition and its parts?

7. Does the recapitulation begin exactly like the opening of the exposition? What differences are there between the recapitulation and the exposition?

8. Is there a coda? If so, how does it relate to the rest of the movement in proportions and function (does it include, for example, further development)? Does the movement end climactically or by "playing itself out"?

II

As we noted in Demonstration 11, the formal aspects of music are influenced by other stylistic

Form
and Function

characteristics; or, putting it another way, the style of a composer includes his particular manner of handling the various structures common to many composers. We observed, for example, in Demonstration 11 that in the chronologically later works the dramatic possibilities of the form came to the fore, particularly in the movements by Schubert, Mendelssohn, and Mahler.

Brahms, *Symphony 3,* first movement, 1883

Listen to the opening of the first movement of Brahms' *Symphony 3;* then compare it with the openings of the earlier symphonic movements discussed in Section I. Consider, first, questions of general character, and notice the striking differences between the opening theme of this movement and the other opening themes. Sing them. Most immediately obvious are the wide range, large leaps, and varied, often irregular rhythm of the Brahms melody. It seems to evolve out of itself, each "bit" growing out of the previous one by subtle manipulation, the process generating one enormously long gesture, in contrast to the clearly articulated (although not necessarily balanced) phrases of the other opening statements.

Perhaps most striking are the differences in Brahms' orchestration and harmony. The "romantic" character of Brahms' opening depends greatly on his use of a large and varied orchestra and his thick, almost muddy texture within which the tone colors of specific instruments, particularly the horns, are exploited. Brahms' use of harmony is often coloristic, bringing the concepts of harmony and sonority very close together. For example, between the first two chords there is an interesting change in color—a major tonic triad followed by a functionally ambiguous chord including the tonic note,

Structure: Process
and Design

184

hinting at the minor mode, and suggesting both tonic and dominant functions by its particular sonority. (These two chords and the third, together with their upper melody line shown in Example 1, pervade the entire movement.) As the large

**Example 1**

gesture continues, major and minor are juxtaposed, along with other chords which exploit the "edges" of the tonality—a kind of chromatic harmony composed of chords not strictly within the key but not changing the tonality, merely enriching and coloring it. The result is a statement of thematic material that is, in comparison with the earlier symphonic movements, unstable, wandering, and charged.

Given this style of grand gesture, enriched harmony, exploitation of instrumental color, and affective, almost associative character, is the sonata form model valid at all? On what level is the generalization possible?

Listen to the rest of the movement asking the questions suggested for the Haydn, Mozart, and Beethoven movements. Notice, for example, the second theme (presented by clarinets and bassoons), with its contrasting character prepared by the transition and a waiting passage. Note the closing passage which evolves out of the contrasting second theme and then by harmonic and motivic manipulation merges into the development. The development section includes a remarkable transformation of the second theme; note also its rapid shifts in key and more active texture. The recapitulation emerges slowly through hints at the familiar motives followed by the two opening

Form
and Function

chords which lead finally into the rebirth of the opening gesture. A long coda is added which includes further development and expansion.

The crucial relationships of the sonata form are thus revealed—almost more as essence than actuality in the light of these changes in style. At the same time we can observe differences in the structure itself—proportions are changed, and the continuous aspects of the form, the areas of organic growth, pervade the entire movement; the functions of the sections are clear but they are rarely delineated by caesurae or cadences; even clearly articulated phrase structure is rare, melodies being characterized by large gestures coalescing out of fragments.

Indeed, it is the notion of the sonata form as sectional which seems to have changed most as we compare this movement with those of Haydn, Mozart, and Beethoven. We are carried along by a process of transformation and change already present in the harmony of the opening chords and in the evolving nature of the first theme. This emphasis on continuous growth together with the associative implications of Brahms' instrumentation and melodic-rhythmic design, generate a "romantic" work in which the course of events, like a narrative, continuously changes our perception of those elements which remain constant.

III

Roger Sessions, *Piano Sonata 2*, first movement, 1946
Bartok, *Sonata for Two Pianos and Percussion*, second movement, 1937
Webern, *Concerto for Nine Instruments*, Opus 24, first movement, 1934
Schoenberg, *Quartet 4*, first movement, 1936

Structure: Process
and Design

These works, all of them written within the last 40 years, are in the most general sense in sonata form. At the same time, the syntax of tonality is to some extent operative only in the piece by Bartok. How, then, can we speak of sonata form, which depends for its very definition on tonal relationships? What is left of the form when the key relationships as well as the concepts of harmonic stability and instability associated with tonality are lacking?

Let us consider one of these movements more closely—Sessions' piano sonata. Listen to the movement several times to see if you can discover, within it, passages of relative stability. (Notice the opening, for example—a motive repeated with slight variation, elaborated to lead to a climax and the statement of another motive.) Hearing these passages in terms of their relative stability is only possible, of course, when you are able to perceive the work in its own terms, without superimposing on it expectations which distort your perception. You will not hear, for example, stability generated by the resolution of dissonance (since resolution implies a triad), or by a dominant–tonic progression establishing a clear tonal center. Remember, however, that in the works we have studied the stability of statement was generated by other means as well, such as a more homophonic texture, or some kind of palpable melodic shape and rhythmic motives which together define a theme. Less stable sections were characterized not only by instability of key but also by a more active texture, conflicts in accent and rhythm, melodic fragmentation, and, in general, a more rapid rate of change. Conclusion was generated often by harmonic stasis but also by a braking action which slowed down the rate of events, reiterating, rather than generating something new. From these characteristics we were able to perceive the function of a passage, and a particular set of relationships among these functions we described as sonata form. In Sessions' sonata we hear the stability of statement generated by many of those attributes which we have associated with thematic statement in music of the past, except that of tonal stability. Similarly, we hear transition, a contrasting second theme, and a closing passage. Development follows the exposition, leading then to a varied recapitulation of the opening material.

While we discovered the relationships of sonata form in the Brahms movement "almost more as essence," the statement is even more true of these twentieth-century pieces. Within styles which are radically different from the styles of the works studied earlier, the idea of sonata form is still operative. By considering the works suggested in Sections I, II, and III (Additional Materials) as a group sharing a common organizing principle, you should become aware of two things: (1) the essential nature of the sonata form and its great flexibility as an organizing principle; and (2) the basic differences in style among the works, particularly as they influence the organization itself.

With these considerations we are to some extent, then, anticipating our concerns in the next chapter, namely, stylistic change in the course of the history of music.


IV

In this chapter our initial distinction between sectional and continuous organization (Chapter 5, Demonstration 7) has become blurred. While it was possible there to juxtapose works in which the distinction is clearly manifest (such as Mozart's *German Dance* and Chopin's prelude), such pieces actually represent the extremes of a continuum in

Structure: Process
and Design

which some works tend more toward one pole than toward the other, and many move in both directions to create contrast and articulate function and design.

One aspect of our initial distinction however, remains to be clarified. We indicated that works described as continuous in organization "defy schematic representation"; that is, they cannot be meaningfully described in terms of some combination of letters (A, B, a, b, etc.). What then can be said of the fugue? Is it not a "form"?

Listen to the following pieces, all of which are fugues. Think about the concept *fugue* as a generalization applicable to these works, compared with the concept *sonata form* as a generalization applicable to the works discussed previously.

Bach, *Cantata 21*, final chorus, 1714
Mozart, *Requiem*, Kyrie, 1791
Beethoven, *Quartet* (*Grosse Fuge*), Opus 133, 1825
Liszt, *Faust Symphony*, Mephistopheles (fugue exposition only), 1854
Brahms, *Variations and Fugue on a Theme by Handel*, fugue, 1861
Bartok, *Music for Strings, Percussion, and Celesta*, first movement, 1936
Hindemith, *Ludus Tonalis*, first fugue, 1942

While it was emphasized in the previous section that the sonata form is an abstraction which each piece realizes uniquely, the design nevertheless does describe the whole work, including at its core an *ordering* of functional relationships: exposition (statement, transition, statement, closing), development, recapitulation, coda. Whatever the common attributes of fugues, on the other hand, their continuous nature precludes (except in the exposition) a generalized ordering of events. Thus the course or design of each fugue is unique. Tovey makes the distinction clear in his definition of fugue: "Fugue is a texture the rules of which do not suffice to determine the shape of the composition as a whole."[3]

For example, notice that in the fugue from *Cantata 21* of Bach the subject is nearly always present, one statement following immediately upon another. Only once before the freer coda do we find an episode. Thus, a normative structural rhythm is established by the length of the subject that is maintained almost throughout the piece. How different from Bach's Fugue no. 3 in C-sharp Major (discussed in Demonstration 13), in which the play between subject statements and episodes is an ever-present source of structural tension! In the fugue from the cantata the omnipresence of the subject itself transfers our attention to the tone color of the particular voice or instrument playing it, the contrasts in density and complexity of texture, and the fashion in which each subject statement emerges out of the total sound fabric.

While the differences in effect between this fugue and the C-sharp Major fugue stem primarily from the spectacular use of chorus and orchestra (with prominent trumpets) in the former, as opposed to the solo harpsichord used in the latter, the particular ordering of events in each fugue is certainly a contributing factor. Indeed, the cantata fugue seems, in our continuum of sectional-continuous organization, much nearer the sectional pole, while the C-sharp Major fugue seems much more continuous.

In listening to the other fugues listed above, notice the following aspects: (1) the relative proportions

[3] Sir Donald Tovey, *The Forms of Music,* Meridian Books, Inc., New York, 1957, p. 36.

Structure: Process
and Design

of subject statements and episodes; (2) the character of the subject itself and how this influences other events in the fugue; (3) the effect of harmonic style (for example, whether the piece is tonal or not); (4) consistency of texture and textural contrasts (for example, in density, complexity, and activity); and (5) the importance of thematic material other than the subject and, indeed, whether more than one subject is developed.

## V

Bach, *Suite 2 in D Minor* (for unaccompanied cello), sarabande, c. 1720

Schoenberg, *Six Little Piano Pieces*, Opus 19, no. 4, 1911

There is another vast body of works found in all historical periods which, even more than the fugue, defy schematic representation. Among these are preludes (such as those we have discussed), fantasies, toccatas, rhapsodies, many so-called "character pieces," other descriptive music such as tone poems, and some overtures. However, we are not concerned with whether a piece does or does not fall into some kind of a schema but rather with your understanding of its internal process—in this case nonperiodic, cumulative or evolving motion, in which structural goals are few and movement between them continuous. Although works so organized can sometimes be described by a schema, the experience of them is such as to make it almost irrelevant.

Listen, for example, to the sarabande from the *Suite 2 in D Minor* by Bach. The sarabande (slow dance) has a traditional binary form: ||:A:||:B:||. But within its two parts it moves continuously forward, the effect being one of organic growth, of constant transformation and evolution. Regularity, in terms of symmetry and periodicity, is obscured by subtle rhythmic transformations and unexpected changes in melodic shape or harmonic direction. Even when a motive is momentarily repeated sequentially, the sequence is broken before it can be taken for granted. On a larger scale there is no sense of return, little feeling of the onward motion turning back upon itself. Even the repeats of each section are hardly heard as such because of the intricacies of the motion. In this context the cadential figure stands out because of its slower, more regular rhythmic and harmonic movement.

Out of the first statement of the cadential figure grow new possibilities for development in the second section: notice, for example, how the rhythmic regularity of the figure appears again in new melodic guise only to be extended, interrupted, and referred to once more but with ambiguous (chromatic) and rapid harmonic motion. The most poignant effect of this continuous development occurs at the moment when the second section reaches the same length as the first. Here there is a tentative cadence in the tonic key, but Bach continues on (A = 12 measures; B = 12 *plus* 4 measures). We move through a momentary sequence reaching the highest melodic point of the piece which becomes, by subtle transformation, the cadential figure bringing the process to rest at last. The powerful individuality of this work makes one hesitate to speak of it as "an example" of anything.

Listen now to the Schoenberg piano piece (heard before as D7.11). Although it moves through three clear phases, it actually manifests a tightly organized process of motivic transformation. Since every detail is significant, it is necessary to listen closely to the piece a number of times in order to grasp its rapid evolution.

The first phase, with its two impulses, establishes the rhythmic and melodic syntax for the whole piece—its significant motives and its bases for tension and resolution. (Note that while this is also true in the Bach sarabande, it is so to a lesser extent because Bach is operating within the broader syntax of tonality and functional harmony. Schoenberg, on the other hand, generates his own syntax out of the materials of the piece itself.) In the second phase the "normative shapes" of Phase 1 are somewhat twisted or turned awry (both melodically and rhythmically), but they remain sufficiently recognizable to provide a sense of evolution, of realization of hidden implications. For example, the sense of a regular beat and meter in the first phase is disrupted in Phase 2 by shifts of accent and fitful motion; the cadential figure in Phase 2, while similar to that of the first phase both melodically and texturally (only at the cadence do we hear chords and notes in the lower register), is rhythmically transformed.

In the third and final phase we hear first a rhythmic compression of the opening melodic motive and then a reminiscence of the "twisted" rhythm of the middle phase ( ♪ ♩. ) which finally reaches resolution in the single-note downbeat that concludes this brief piece.

Paradoxically, although all three phases are nearly equal in length, the events are so different in each that the effect is not one of balanced structure at all! The experience of continuous movement despite caesurae and balance might be compared with the sense of continuous movement achieved in the sarabande, in spite of the two repeated sections. What about the brevity of this piece? It has taken you much longer to read this description than to listen to the piece, which takes approximately 20 seconds to play. This compression is a significant factor in generating the effect of the piece as a single impulsive gesture, but one so tightly organized that every instant is significant to the process—nothing is redundant.

VI

In the light of your careful study of the two works in Section V, you will probably find it interesting to go back and listen to the other works that we touched upon briefly in previous discussions of continuous organization (see Chapter 5, Additional Materials):

Palestrina, *Missa Aeterna Christi munera,* Sanctus
Purcell, *Dido and Aeneas,* Dido's Lament
Wagner, *Tristan und Isolde,* prelude
Palestrina, *Missa In festis Apostolorum,* Kyrie (D7.5)
Bach, *Two-Part Invention in F Major,* no. 8 (D7.6)
Froberger, *Toccata 2* (D7.7)
Bach, *St. Matthew Passion,* aria (D7.12)
Stravinsky, *Le Sacre du printemps,* beginning (D7.13)

The
Historical
Context

*Nijinsky as Petrouchka*
Miriam Brofsky, 1963
(Collection, Mr. and Mrs. Bernard Katz)

# STYLE AND MUSIC HISTORY: A MODEL OF PROCEDURE *8*

At this juncture we add another dimension to our study—that of style and music history. While an awareness of stylistic differences may have been a by-product of the work you have done up to this point, it is only now that we will focus on it directly. In this chapter we propose a model of procedure by studying in depth the period from 1860 to 1913. Then in the last chapter (Chapter 9), we provide you with a skeletal outline of music history referring to examples heard previously but now rearranged chronologically to illustrate generalizations about the style of each period. This outline will serve as a reference and a framework for further study.[1]

The term "style" refers to that complex of characteristics which stamps the music of a particular composer or era. A composer's style is, in fact, a set of implicit norms, assumptions, and unique characteristics which allows you to say, even when

[1] Please note that in Chapter 8 the musical examples discussed are not included in the accompanying records. Since the discussion in most cases is more general than in previous chapters (referring, for example, to sections of an entire movement of a symphony or to a scene from an opera), you will find it necessary to use a recording of the complete work. It should be emphasized that the discussion here as elsewhere in the book will have little meaning if the reader is not also a listener.

you turn on the radio in the middle of a work, "Ah, Bach!" or "That's Brahms!" How do you know? We are not concerned here with identification—which can become a game substituting for, or at least interfering with, the experience of the unique work in its totality. Rather we are concerned with a kind of flexibility in listening, at times approaching virtuosity, which allows you to shift your focus, to move freely from one period to another, perceiving as configurations and events those which are appropriate to the piece in question—that is, to involve yourself with the work on its own terms.

This brief discussion of style brings us to the many problems and questions of music history, which on its simplest level deals with the changes of style that have taken place over a period of time. We can in the context of this book merely enumerate some of these problems, and in our detailed model of procedure touch on some of the answers.

1. Since the style of an era encompasses the individual differences of many composers, what is the relationship between the individual and the style? In earlier periods are individual differences fewer; that is, can we speak more readily of a "common practice," or are the apparent similarities in style due only to chronological distance?

2. How important is critical evaluation, during and after their times, of composers within a specific era? For example, our excerpts from the Classical Period are drawn only from Haydn, Mozart, and Beethoven; what about the music of their "lesser" contemporaries and its relationship to the style of the period? In the late Baroque Period, the composer Telemann was generally held in higher esteem than J. S. Bach, yet today we hear hardly any of Telemann's music.

The Historical
Context

3. Can we or should we try to listen with, let us say, "eighteenth-century ears" to eighteenth-century music? Our understanding of a period means that we have determined and are in some respects sensitive to its normative procedures, for example, the function of passages within a sonata form movement of the late eighteenth century. But how can we shut out the sounds of two subsequent centuries of music? For example, could we possibly hope to recapture the feeling that a sensitive listener must have experienced hearing for the first time the beginning of the development section of the last movement of Mozart's *Symphony 40?* Our reaction to this tremendous shock to the tonal system is of course tempered by our experience of the subsequent expansion and ultimate dissolution of tonality as a fundamental force.

4. How do styles change from one period to another, and can we determine causal factors?

5. Can we speak meaningfully of interrelationships among the arts at a particular time? Can we transfer our generalizations about music to contemporaneous activities in art and literature? And how do we make this kind of transfer to a very different art? Is there a "time lag" between one art and another? If so, when and why?

6. Finally, what is the relationship between music and society? What role do sociological and economic factors play in the history of an art? What is the relationship between the artist and his audience? Do the attitudes and tastes of the audience influence the composer's work? To pose only one question here: what about music written on the turbulent eve of the French Revolution? Mozart and Haydn were the leading composers!

Style and Music
History

While we are posing fundamental questions about the interpretation of history, its events, and their resultant "objects," partial answers can be found within your own experience thus far. In previous chapters we have juxtaposed works irrespective of their dates of composition, often to demonstrate *similarities*. In Chapter 7 we proceeded chronologically, demonstrating change within a framework of certain structural *constants*. Now, in regrouping chronologically the previously heard examples, we are adding another dimension—that of a composition as an historical "object" existing within a body of other objects bearing some relationship to it. From your own experience of these works it should be clear, then, that the flexibility of perception we have referred to above does not imply assuming a totally new stance when listening to pieces written at different times and in different styles. Some aspects of musical organization are relevant to all music; the questions are "which" and "when." Listening to a work on its own terms, then, assumes both the ability to perceive the various possibilities we have discussed earlier in this book and an awareness of the particular manner in which a composer manipulates and plays with these possibilities. Expanding and using this awareness in reference to works written within a given period will create a sense of historical context.

The chronological regrouping of examples in Chapter 9 calls for a cautionary note. In keeping with the fundamental approach of this book, the *experience* of the pieces themselves should precede the discussion and acquisition of "data." Because the examples are for the most part excerpts from larger works, you should now listen to the entire work in order to comprehend the whole. Even a rehearing of the excerpts alone in this new chronological context, however, should enable you to derive some sense of the style of the era. You should go back and listen to and reread the discussions of the examples. Consider where each example occurred and what it illustrated.

The stylistic generalizations we make about a period are based primarily on these excerpts. Since they were chosen with other purposes in mind, it follows that they may not be the most "representative" works, that they may not give a complete picture of the period (were this possible within a limited time and space, and without superficiality). This problem is particularly evident in the earlier periods, and therefore we will suggest additional listening to enable you to "cover" a period more adequately. As mentioned above, the detailed discussion of the period from 1860 to 1913 which follows should serve as a model for your study of other periods.

## Suggested Reading

Any one of the three general histories of music listed below can be highly recommended for its comprehensive coverage. The books differ somewhat in approach; the first two contain more analyses of individual works, and the third provides a broader cultural background.

Crocker, Richard L., *A History of Musical Style*, McGraw-Hill, New York, 1966.

Grout, Donald, *A History of Western Music*, Norton, New York, 1960.

Lang, Paul Henry, *Music in Western Civilization*, Norton, New York, 1941.

# A Model for the Study
## of Musical Style and History
### 1860 to 1913

The study of a specific period in music history can require a year-long course, a week or two in a survey course, or the lifetime of a musicologist. Here we present a model for procedure in such a study. Our discussion will be confined to music written during the latter half of the nineteenth and the early part of the twentieth century, and we will focus on only a few significant works, pointing out what we take to be the two main trends during this period. Thus we continue to emphasize personal experience—this time your experience of specific works as you hear them within their historical context. In order to gain a larger perspective on the period under discussion, you should, in addition to "immersing" yourself in the music of the period, read selectively from among the books suggested in the bibliography at the end of this chapter.

We have chosen the period from about 1860 to the outbreak of World War I because within it stylistic contrast is often marked and thus can be easily perceived. Conversely, a sensitivity to stylistic change becomes important in listening to the music of this time precisely because of its growing diversity. In some senses also, this period provides guides to the greater difficulties of the music of our own era.

Listen first to two works written at either end of the period.

Wagner, *Tristan und Isolde*, Act II, scene 2 (composed 1857–1859; first performance, 1865)
Schoenberg, *Pierrot lunaire*, first song, Mondestrunken, 1912

The Historical
Context

How would you describe the fundamental differences in style between these two works? Implicit in this question is another: What fundamental means does each composer use to make his work comprehensible? Or, more important for our purposes, what specific assumptions must the listener make if he is to respond appropriately to each work?

The listener must shift his focus, must demonstrate the kind of listening flexibility we have emphasized if he is to comprehend both the Wagner and the Schoenberg works. If he clings to the assumptions inherent in the Wagner piece, he may find the Schoenberg work incomprehensible (consider only the harmonic assumptions, for example). Thus, two more questions arise: (1) how does the listener achieve this essential flexibility, and (2) what sort of historical process occurred between Wagner and Schoenberg? Can the first question be resolved by listening to the earlier work first; will listening to Wagner's *Tristan* then make the Schoenberg piece more intelligible? In other words, is there a natural stylistic evolution which, if experienced, makes the various phases of music history understandable? Can the history of music, then, be described in terms of influences and orderly transformations? And if it can, how important is the individual composer (with his own history, his own private consciousness) or the individual composition (with its own history and its own set of internal events)?

To emphasize these problems, consider two more works also written at the limits of our selected time span.

Moussorgsky, *Boris Godunov,* coronation scene (composed 1868–1872; first performance, 1874)
Stravinsky, *Le Sacre du printemps,* Dance of the Adolescents, 1913

Then listen to the four examples again and consider how you would pair them, using similarity of style as a basis. Will you pair them by date of composition—the two nineteenth-century works and the two twentieth-century works? Or by nationality—two German composers and two Russian composers?

It seems immediately clear that the greatest similarity is between the last two works—both by Russian composers. What characteristics do these pieces have in common? Listen to them again noticing the following similarities.

1.  An insistent sonority (particular combination of pitches) which pervades the "pitch atmosphere"—in Moussorgsky's work, the alternation of two chords from the traditional tonal repertoire, here no longer functionally (tonally) related; and in Stravinsky's a single chord which is a nontriadic combination of pitches (nonfunctional in the traditional sense).
2.  A persistent beat, metrically regular in Moussorgsky's piece but much less so in Stravinsky's.
3.  An exploitation of instrumental color for its own sake.
4.  *Juxtaposition* of sections rather than *transition* between them.
5.  Folk-like melodies which are modal rather than tonal in their pitch organization, and which are often simply repeated with different orchestration (or voices), rather than developed.

While the Wagner and Schoenberg examples are less strikingly similar, they are more like each other than like either of the other pieces. For example, they have the following traits in common.

1.  An effect of intensity bordering on hysteria.
2.  The use of melodic motives as the basic source of

unity (rather than the persistent sonority used by Moussorgsky and Stravinsky).

3. The manipulation of these motives through sequence, imitation, and other techniques.
4. A sense of continuous development achieved in part by motivic manipulation, and including transition rather than juxtaposition as a means of moving from one section to another.
5. An absence of clear phrases due to the motivic nature of the melodic lines and to overlapping among the parts.
6. An active texture, with parts struggling against one another to be heard.
7. A large range in both the instrumental and vocal parts.
8. A sense of *structural rhythm,* generated by chord changes, the length of the motives, and the pace of motivic repetition, rather than a prominence of the beat per se. (The sense of pulse, in fact, is quite subordinate in Wagner's and Schoenberg's music.)

In pairing these four works we have demonstrated the two major and contrasting stylistic trends which emerged during the latter half of the nineteenth and the beginning of the twentieth century. While change takes place within these two groups (as the examples themselves demonstrate), the differences which we have observed in these four examples remain to distinguish German and Russian music throughout the period. We will continue our discussion, then, by pursuing these two trends individually, finally bringing them back together to consider the changes that have occurred.

## FROM WAGNER
## TO SCHOENBERG

As we narrow our area of discussion to the Austro-German composers, differences (which may appear

*Johannes Brahms (at about 33)*

small in a larger context) emerge even between two composers who were writing contemporaneously. Indeed, in the case of Brahms and Wagner these differences became a "cause célèbre."[2]

I

Listen to the first movement of Brahms' *Third Symphony* (see also Chapter 7, Additional Materials), and compare it with the Liebestod ("Love-Death") from Wagner's *Tristan und Isolde*.

Brahms, *Symphony 3*, first movement, 1883
Wagner, *Tristan und Isolde*, Liebestod, 1857–1859

[2]See Donald F. Tovey, *The Forms of Music*, Meridian Books, Inc., New York, 1957, pp. 128–132; and Gerald Abraham, *A Hundred Years of Music*, 3rd ed., Aldine, Chicago, 1964, pp. 129–132.

The Historical
Context

Brahms wrote no operas, Wagner no symphonies. Inherent in this fact is a fundamental difference in approach. For example, Brahms' *Symphony 3* falls into the traditional four movements, each of which in some way embodies a traditional organizing principle (such as sonata form or ABA). On a more detailed level, you will remember from our discussion of Brahms' first movement that its structure was realized through contrasts in the functions of sections: statements (generally in one key with a relatively clear melodic shape), transitions (modulatory and more fragmented melodically), elaborations and development, and cadential passages. In addition the statement passages differ in character, providing another kind of contrast. Thus, while Brahms' harmonic, instrumental, and rhythmic means may be different from, for instance, Beethoven's, one still responds to those structural functions which generate drama in purely musical terms.

Wagner, on the other hand, developed means of organization which derived, to a large extent, from the drama of his text. Thus in the Liebestod we are swept along both musically and dramatically (love-death) in a process of transformation. Even the traditional divisions of opera (aria, recitative, and such) are no longer heard in this music. Wagner writes continuous music—"endless melody"—in which there is sequential development of "significant motives" (usually associated with a character or idea) in a complex, often highly active texture characterized by continuous modulation and avoidance of cadences. In addition to the constant shifting and merging of tonal centers, the harmonic implications of chords are often diverted or left unfulfilled. Specifically, the dominant seventh chord (the crux of the tension-building waiting passages of Beethoven and Rossini; see

Style and Music
History

Demonstration 10) is frequently heard as stable. It resolves more ambiguous harmonic movement by momentarily defining or pointing to a specific key. The result is music that is continuously searching, building, surging toward a climax. How different from the carefully contrasted passages, each with its own function, that we hear in Brahms.

Brahms, *Alto Rhapsody,* Opus 53, 1869

Listening to the *Alto Rhapsody,* however, one recognizes that Brahms and Wagner are indeed contemporaneous. Given a text describing an unhappy youth wandering through a desolate, wintry landscape, Brahms writes music in which broader expressive means are explored. The harmony, like Wagner's, is more chromatic; cadences are avoided and sectionalism is therefore abandoned; the mood is unified; and, in a sense, specific demands on our rationality are relatively suspended. This is dramatic music, but without the near hysteria of the Wagner excerpt and with the singer given a more predominant role.

Thus we see that it is the *genre* rather than the date of composition that brings these two composers stylistically closer together. In Chapter 7 we suggested that traditional forms became more dramatic in the nineteenth century; but set alongside Wagner, Brahms now appears rather closer to tradition in these instrumental works. It was when Brahms turned to music inspired by and expressive of a text that we hear him exploring other musical dimensions. What then constitutes drama in Brahms' symphonic movements as compared with drama in his vocal works?

II

Mahler, *Das Lied von der Erde,* no. 2, "Autumn Loneliness," 1908

*Gustav Mahler*
Auguste Rodin
(Rodin Museum, Philadelphia
Museum of Art)

This song for voice and orchestra, written 39 years after Brahms' *Alto Rhapsody*, at first sounds almost like a continuation of that piece. The affinity between the two songs lies in their clear, largely diatonic, melody lines, which soar above a relatively thin orchestral texture; the rich harmony of the accompaniment with its elusive cadences; and the single, poignant mood of the text from which the continuous musical structure derives.

Paradoxically Mahler, who considered himself in the Wagner camp, deprecated Brahms' music: "All I can say of him is that he's a puny little dwarf with a rather narrow chest. . . . It is very seldom he can make anything whatever of his themes, beautiful as they often are. Only Beethoven and Wagner, after all, could do that."[3] (Of course, it should be remembered that Mahler was speaking here primarily of Brahms' symphonies rather than

[3] From a letter to his wife, written June 23, 1904; quoted in Irving Kolodin, ed., *The Composer as Listener*, Collier, New York, 1958, p. 51.

Style and Music
History

of his dramatic vocal music.) But despite Mahler's devotion to the music of Wagner, his style differs from Wagner's in that he does not create a "competition" between voice and orchestra; his orchestra lacks Wagner's thick, active texture in which the instruments merge into a mass of sound; nor do we hear in Mahler Wagner's constant surging toward an ever-bigger climax.

Mahler, *Symphony 1,* first movement, 1888

Similarity of genre, however, need not result in similarity of style. Mahler's *Symphony 1* was written only five years after Brahms' *Symphony 3,* yet the differences between them are striking. Mahler, unlike Brahms, tended to be influenced by extra-musical associations even in his symphonies. His *Symphony 1* is subtitled "The Titan"; many of his later ones have programmatic associations, and often text and voice are introduced; traditional forms, present in a freer guise (see D11.7), are greatly expanded and do not have the same sense of the classical tradition found in Brahms. Notice in listening to the first movement of Mahler's *Symphony 1* the large orchestra and extensive use of horns, trumpets, and even woodwinds at the top of their registers; the very active texture which is yet so transparent that one seems able to hear clearly each instrumental color. The melodies are sometimes folk-like and strongly diatonic, sometimes more chromatic and Wagnerian; the pulse is strong, often emphasized by timpani. The jubilant mood is created in part by tossing these melodies through the orchestra, combining them, fragmenting them, and juxtaposing them with abandon. Mahler himself described this process in terms of his use of ". . . *themes*—clear and *plastic,* so that they are distinctly recognizable in every transformation and further unfolding; then a working out, full of variety, and, above all, gripping because of the *development* of the inner idea and also because of the *genuine opposition* of the motifs placed in contrast to each other."[4]


## III

Richard Strauss, *Don Juan*, 1888

Mahler described Richard Strauss as a "literary man" and the majority of Strauss' works are programmatic in some sense. In the same year that Mahler wrote his *Symphony 1*, Strauss composed a "tone poem"—an orchestral work in one movement inspired by a poem, "Don Juan," by the Hungarian poet, Nikolaus Lenau. The character of the Don "on a gallant hunt for womanly perfection" is immediately portrayed in the music by its huge melodic range (so different from Mahler's folk-like melodies), its martial rhythmic patterns, the use of brass in a characteristic fanfare manner, and the massive orchestra and thick texture out of which melodies and instruments seem to struggle for individual existence. As the tone poem progresses, notice how themes of strongly contrasting character rapidly succeed one another (for example, a momentary dance melody, the Don's theme, and eventually a "feminine" solo violin melody). Thus, structure is generated largely by extramusical events and characters with which particular themes, instruments, and rhythms are associated. The music is more chromatic than Mahler's, full of contrast and yet nonsectional in the classical sense, freely evolving through the manipulation, juxtaposition, and intertwining of thematic material.

[4]Gustav Mahler, *Briefe*, p. 191, quoted in William A. Austin, *Music in the 20th Century*, Norton, New York, 1966, p. 129.

Style and Music
History

*Richard Strauss*

Richard Strauss, *Elektra,* 1909

We turn now to an opera by Strauss. Listen to Elektra's soliloquy on the death of her murdered father.

Strauss, like Brahms, pushes his musical vocabulary to its extremes in the service of his text. *Elektra,* written 21 years after *Don Juan,* reveals a considerably extended chromaticism (a single tonal center is never maintained); a melodic line that is often sharply disjunct, with a range that puts the most extreme demands on the singer; and a relationship between singer and orchestra that varies from a kind of accompanied recitative to an almost Wagnerian struggle between voice and instruments. All this is designed to express the intense, nearly insane emotion of the singer. Imagine

Mahler choosing the story of Elektra as a subject for a piece of music!

IV

Schoenberg, *Transfigured Night,* 1899

Schoenberg's *Transfigured Night* was written 10 years earlier and clearly goes back still further to Wagner for its musical ancestry. The surging climaxes; thick, turbulent texture; chromatic harmony; motivic manipulation; unified mood; and even the motives themselves are particularly reminiscent of *Tristan und Isolde.* A jury that reviewed the piece for possible performance declared: "It sounds as if one had smeared over the still moist Tristan score."[5]

With this early work of Schoenberg we approach the last phase in our study of Austro-German works up to World War I. It has provided only a tourist's view; the traveler needs to spend more time if he is to understand fully where he has been. The remaining works, all by Schoenberg, give us the opportunity to consider the style of a single composer. The notion of evolutionary change might thus seem less problematic; Schoenberg's stylistic transformation, however, is quite remarkable over this period of 13 years. While his essays and letters describe his personal struggle for what he considered "necessary" means of expression,[6] his works themselves are equally, perhaps more, revealing.

[5] The Vienna *Tonkünstlerverein* jury (which refused performance of the work); in Sam Morgenstern, ed., *Composers on Music,* Pantheon, New York, 1956, p. 377.

[6] See especially Schoenberg's essay, "Composition with 12 Tones," in Arnold Schoenberg, *Style and Idea,* Dika Newlin, trans. and ed., Philosophical Library, New York, 1950.

*Arnold Schoenberg*
Self-portrait
(Belmont Music Publishers, Los Angeles)

Schoenberg, *Chamber Symphony 1 in E Major,* Opus 9, 1906

This symphony, written 7 years after *Transfigured Night,* is scored for 15 solo instruments. The charged atmosphere, reminiscent of the earlier work, requires the utmost from each instrument in the unique ensemble. The two pieces are also similar in their extensive use of a few motives— rather than clear, palpable melodies—and in their constant manipulation of them. The music is continuously developmental. In the following excerpt Schoenberg discusses the composition of this work.[7]

[7]"Heart and Brain" in *Style and Idea,* p. 162.

The Historical
Context

There was at hand from the start a sufficient amount of motival forms and their derivatives, rather too much than too little. The task, therefore, was to retard the progress of development in order to enable the average good listener to keep in mind what preceded so as to understand the consequences. To keep within bounds and to balance a theme whose character, tempo, expression, harmonic progression, and motival contents displayed a centrifugal tendency: this was here the task.

The striking difference between the two works lies in the curious mixture of new and old found in the *Chamber Symphony:* tonality is still operative (notice the full cadence at the end of the brief introductory passage), but almost as if it were struggling for existence under an attack of extreme chromaticism. Coupled with this is a wildly active texture in which angular, even jagged motives overlap, interrupt, and intrude on one another. Rhythm depends on the length of motives, pace of attack, and harmonic change rather than on pulse or meter, which are often submerged. The ascending chain of fourths in the horn near the beginning of the piece is used as a basis for new chord formations based on the interval of the fourth rather than the third. Solo instruments are used to create a complex but transparent texture which becomes increasingly significant in Schoenberg's music. The dramatic intensity of the piece lies not in a program but in more purely musical processes—for example, the transformations of a few motives, the movement from solo statement to increasing textural density and activity, and the dissolution to solo statement again. The strangely anguished quality of the piece seems to lie partly in its struggle with past means of comprehensibility, with past assumptions which are being pushed to their limits. The music is thus both decadent and explosive!

Style and Music
History

Schoenberg, *Five Pieces for Orchestra,* Opus 16, no. 1, 1909

Three years later, Schoenberg had created a new musical world, a world that has had its effect on every subsequent composer. Perhaps most immediately evident in this music is its extreme brevity, its sense of condensed action. Schoenberg says of the works of this period,[8]

The first compositions in this new style were written by me around 1908 and, soon afterwards, by my pupils Anton von Webern and Alban Berg. From the very beginning such compositions differed from all preceding music, not only harmonically but also melodically, thematically and motivally. But the foremost characteristics of those pieces *in statu nascendi* were their extreme expressiveness and their extraordinary brevity. At that time, neither I nor my pupils were conscious of the reasons for these features. Later I discovered that our sense of form was right when it forced us to counterbalance extreme emotionality with extraordinary shortness. Thus, subconsciously consequences were drawn from an innovation which, like every innovation, destroys while it produces. New colorful harmony was offered; but much was lost.

Harmonically, this work seems to have burst the limits which we were so acutely aware of in the *Chamber Symphony.* Schoenberg ascribes the difference to the "emancipation of the dissonance":[9]

The term *emancipation of the dissonance* refers to its comprehensibility, which is considered equivalent to the consonance's comprehensibility. A style based on this premise treats dissonances like consonances and renounces a tonal center. By avoiding the establishment

[8]"Composition with 12 Tones," in *Style and Idea,* p. 105.
[9]*Ibid.*

of a key, modulation is excluded, since modulation means leaving an established tonality and establishing *another* tonality.

In this music melody and harmony as previously understood are highly fragmented, almost shattered; the awareness of specific melodic and rhythmic motives thus becomes crucial to grasping the logic of the piece. In the midst of a complex counterpoint we hear strong, terse, constantly evolving melodic fragments, sometimes sounding against a repeated figure in the bass and occurring

*Anton Webern*
Oskar Kokoschka
(Collection Annie Knize, New York)

Style and Music
History

217

in a vast array of slightly varied, interconnected shapes and instrumental colors. The large orchestra is treated almost like a group of solo instruments, as in the *Chamber Symphony,* allowing the highly intricate detail to emerge. Through manipulation and contrast of rhythmic and textural activity, the structure seems to develop out of itself with the "logic" of free association. The overall effect is one of tremendous energy and vitality—alive and fresh rather than decadent; self-contained rather than explosive.

Schoenberg, *Quartet 2 in F-sharp Minor,* third movement, 1910

In this quartet Schoenberg introduces the voice into the string quartet—another invasion of the instrumental realm. Schoenberg writes:[10]

. . . it seemed at first impossible to compose pieces of complicated organization or of great length. A little later I discovered how to construct larger forms by following a text or poem. The differences in size and shape of its parts and the change in character and mood were mirrored in the shape and size of the composition, in its dynamics and tempo, figuration and accentuation, instrumentation and orchestration. Thus the parts were differentiated as clearly as they had formerly been by the tonal and structural functions of harmony.

This movement from the *Second Quartet* is somewhat reminiscent of *Elektra* in the great demands made on the singer, the wide range, the very disjunct melody, and the quest for climaxes. But unlike Strauss, Schoenberg uses a limited number of instruments, exploiting their possibilities in new ways and creating a texture which is relatively thin and transparent but rich in coloristic effect.

[10] *Ibid.,* p. 106.

Throughout we hear Schoenberg reaching for the extremes to create an effect of intense emotional expression.

V

Schoenberg, *Pierrot lunaire,* Mondestrunken, 1912

We arrive at the end of our study of German and Austrian music with one of the masterpieces of the twentieth century. In *Pierrot lunaire* Schoenberg brings together in the most concentrated form all the aspects of his music that we have heard emerging in his earlier works. The bizarre, almost frightening atmosphere of the text (by the Belgian poet Albert Giraud) is reflected in every detail of the music. Combining singing and speaking (*sprechstimme*) the singer penetrates the atmosphere portraying the madness of a moonstruck clown.

Despite the effect of hysteria, the music unfolds with an intense, tight logic. Scored for only five players and eight instruments (piano, flute and piccolo, clarinet and bass clarinet, violin and viola, and cello), the song develops, with an extreme concentration of detail, out of initial motives which the composer transforms to reflect the text. Notice, for example, the "waves" created by a sequentially repeated motive played transparently by the flute, violin *pizzicato,* and the upper register of the piano: "pours from the moon in waves at nightfall." This passage is in immediate contrast to a thick, active texture in which the cello enters and the motive moves within the predominant sound of percussive low piano chords: "The poet by his ardor driven."

Perhaps the most remarkable aspect of this piece historically is that in it Schoenberg, incorporating

Style and Music
History

219

many of the characteristics of his earlier style (so clearly influenced by the Austro-German composers of the late nineteenth century), has spawned something entirely new. Schoenberg's stylistic change over this period of 13 years includes both what he termed the "dissolution of tonality" and the creation of fresh bases for organizing pitch, the full implications of which were realized only in the years following 1914. The particular means which Schoenberg found are inextricably bound in with the stylistic characteristics of the Austro-German tradition, as will become even clearer when we consider the quite different style of Stravinsky and his predecessors. You may find it interesting now to go back to the first Wagner examples and listen to them now in the light of your awareness of later developments in German and Austrian music.

## FROM MOUSSORGSKY TO STRAVINSKY

In our earlier discussion we noticed a rather striking similarity between the two Russian composers who delimit our time period—Moussorgsky and Stravinsky. Indeed, on first hearing there seemed to be more in common between them than between the two German composers; their similarities suggest a clear stylistic tradition in the Russian music of this period.

The more easily heard similarity between the two Russian works as compared with the German (*Tristan* and *Pierrot lunaire*) is significant in considering the stylistic traditions of each country. We might say that the "surface," the "face" of German music changed radically during these 50 years, while certain less immediately accessible characteristics (such as structural process) remained to define the tradition. In Russian music the surface remains recognizable, and it is this more obvious quality that is crucial in defining the style.

Another body of music, that of France, is closely related to the Russian music of this period. The cultural affinity between Russia and France during the late nineteenth century was evidenced in many ways. Members of the Russian aristocracy spoke French as a second language. The intellectual, artistic, and social elite traveled frequently between the two countries (Debussy worked for some months in Moscow in his early years). A certain revolutionary spirit was shared by some Russian and French intellectuals. This relationship comes alive in the novels of Tolstoy, Dostoevski, and Turgenev and in the plays of Chekov.

I

Musically, this affinity is immediately evident. Listen to the openings of the following works:

Moussorgsky, *Khovantchina*, prelude, 1873–1881
Debussy, *Prélude à l'Après-midi d'un Faune,* 1894
Debussy, *Iberia*, Parfums de la Nuit, 1906–1909
Stravinsky, *Le Sacre du printemps,* 1913

What contributes to the characteristic sound of these works? They are rhythmically amorphous, haunted by the changing color of solo instruments (particularly winds) set against a background texture which is mobile, often shimmering and nebulous. We are drawn into a musical world in which the play of sounds itself is the prime source of pleasure. Although differences will emerge as we study the period and the individual works of

Style and Music
History

221

*Modest Moussorgsky*
Il'ya Yefimovich Repin
(Sovfoto, New York)

Russian and French composers, these qualities persist. Indeed, they make it possible to speak of a Russian-French tradition.

Our approach to this music will be somewhat different from that used in examining the music of Germany and Austria. Instead of treating the period strictly chronologically, we will focus on the common threads that recur. We will make a series of temporal sweeps, rather than temporal steps, first within Russian and then within French music.

II

Moussorgsky, *Khovantchina*, prelude, 1873–1881
Moussorgsky, *Boris Godunov*, prologue, 1868–1872

The Historical
Context

Moussorgsky, *Pictures at an Exhibition,* Polish Oxcart,
  Great Gate of Kiev, 1874
Borodin, *Prince Igor,* Polovetsian Dances, 1869–1887
Stravinsky, *Firebird Suite,* finale, 1910
Stravinsky, *Petrouchka,* Part I, 1911

In these examples a new element appears: a pervasive sense of Russia. Nationalism was a powerful factor guiding and inspiring a group of Russian composers known as the Mighty Five—Moussorgsky, Borodin, Rimsky-Korsakov, Cui, and Balakirev. Seeking out Russian history, myth, and folk song, they tried to free themselves from foreign (especially German) influence in order to create a music that was truly Russian. Their aggressive, almost violent anti-German feelings are expressed by Moussorgsky in the following remarks, written to two young ladies requesting information about German songs:[11]

Of the German things sing the ones you like, because it's better for you to make the choice *accidentally,* than for me—at a distance: *accidentally,* for I am very doubtful about German vocal music in particular. German men and women sing like roosters, imagining that the more their mouths gape and the longer they hold their notes, the more feeling they show. To speak harshly, *Kartoffel, Kirschensuppe, Milch* and *Tchernickensuppe* do not have an especially good influence on the power of feeling and particularly on artistic feeling, and for my taste the Germans, moving from their leather fried in pork-fat to the seven-hour operas of Wagner, offer nothing attractive for me.

Most important to this group of composers was the extensive use of Russian folk melodies or com-

[11]Letter to Alexandra and Nadezhda Purgeld, written June 20, 1870 in Petrograd; in Jay Leyda and Sergei Bertensson, eds. and trans., *The Musorgsky Reader,* Norton, New York, 1947, p. 138.

posed folk-like melodies. Cesar Cui describes the attributes of the Russian folk song as follows:[12]

One of the principal elements in the structure of Russian song is the complete freedom of rhythm, carried to the point of caprice. Not only may the musical phrases be composed of an unequal number of measures, but even in the same song the rhythm of the measures may change several times. These changing rhythms are, above all, *right*, since they are supremely expressive. At the same time, they utterly exclude the impression of banality and monotony which sometimes results from the prolonged use of a uniform and overworked rhythm.

But their very variety is such that an unpracticed ear does not grasp certain Russian songs clearly, as long as the musical phrases are not divided and established into precise measures. Another notable fact is . . . that very often, the theme is not constructed on the current European scale, but on old Greek modes, the origin of church music. . . . The use of the Greek modes . . . has the further advantage of a great diversity because, in Greek music, the position of the half steps varies with each mode, while in European music it is fixed.

The Russian folk song imperiously demands an original harmonization and a very special art of modulation. First, it is rare to come on a song the melody of which can be treated entirely in one of the two modes, major or minor; most often, even if it spans but a few measures, it passes from the minor to its relative major and vice versa.

It also happens that the harmony of a single chord remains stationary throughout an entire song, which lends it an overall quality of vague melancholy, a complexion of deliberate monotony.

Russian folk tunes are ordinarily confined within a very restricted note-span, only rarely exceeding the interval

[12]Cesar Cui, from *La Musique en Russie*, quoted in Morgenstern, ed., *Composers on Music*, pp. 220–225.

The Historical
Context

of a fifth or sixth. . . . The theme is always short; some are limited to two measures, but these measures are repeated as many times as the scope of the text demands.

Cui's comments quite accurately describe the unique qualities of the melodies we heard in the previous examples.

A characteristic process of organization, stemming in part from the use of folk song, is found throughout these works. Sectional in the larger sense, they proceed from one part to another by juxtaposition rather than by transition. (Notice the difference in this respect between the excerpts from *Boris Godunov* and *Tristan und Isolde,* or between *Pictures at an Exhibition* and the movement from Brahms' *Symphony 3.*) Within the parts we hear clear smaller sections created often by the repetition of whole melodies which are varied largely by orchestration and texture rather than by transformation or motivic elaboration.

Indeed, one of the crucial differences between Russian and German compositions of this period lies precisely in the concept of development. In the German music we noticed an emphasis on what we called "organic growth": the manipulation of a motivic germ to create passages of varying structural functions, climax, dissolution, and so forth. In Russian music, melodies tend to remain intact; development then consists of exploiting a variety of coloristic and textural possibilities while melodic and harmonic relationships remain relatively constant within any one section.

On the other hand, the fluid and elusive structure of the melodies themselves, as described by Cui, generates a kind of mobility within stasis. For example, the *Khovantchina* melody (which is

Style and Music
History

225

stated after the introduction), especially the ordering of its various phrases, is difficult to remember.
The wandering quality of this melody contributes
to the prelude's sense of mobility in spite of the
many repetitions.

III

Perhaps most important to the sense of contained
mobility in these pieces is their remarkable variety
and richness of texture and, even more striking, the
use of strange and wonderful instrumental colors.
Listen to these works again, along with those listed
below, noticing particularly the way in which the
composers change the character of a melody or
a chord by altering its instrumentation and its
sonorous surroundings.

Rimsky-Korsakov, *Capriccio Espagnol,* variations, 1887
Stravinsky, *Le Sacre du printemps,* Dance of the Adoles-
    cents, 1913

Harmony (chord relationships) is tied very closely
to color and sonority in these examples. A particular combination of tones (a chord) is often used
to imitate the sound of an object (bells or a circus)
or to evoke an image (dancing adolescents). Consider specifically the opening of the coronation
scene in *Boris Godunov* and the Dance of the
Adolescents from *Le Sacre du printemps.* Both
make use of a particular and unique chordal sonority rather than a harmonic syntax (a framework in
which tension, resolution, direction, or goal is
implicit). In the coronation scene there are two
chords which move only by alternating with one
another. Each is, in itself, a familiar combination
of tones; but juxtaposed they neither imply a particular tonal center nor create harmonic direction or
even tonal ambiguity. Harmonically, the passage is

static. Compare this opening, for example, with the opening of the *Tristan* prelude. The situation is almost the opposite. In the prelude there is directed harmonic motion—goals are implied; tension is created because the direction shifts and the goals are avoided. In *Le Sacre du printemps* as in *Boris Godunov*, a particular sonority is used, but it is different in nature: it is not triadic. To this factor and its historical significance we will return shortly.

There is a crucial connection here between harmonic and structural style, just as there was between melodic style and structure. The fact that we feel little sense of built-in directed harmonic movement is inextricably related to our sense of an additive structure. Each section is contained by its relatively static harmony; motion within it derives primarily from coloristic and textural variation. Chords, then, become a part of the dimension of color; they are sensuous entities to be embellished and enjoyed rather than elements in a complex of interrelated functions.

This harmonic stasis is animated rhythmically as well as melodically and texturally. For example, the coronation scene moves (within its limits) through an increase in rhythmic activity. While the beat remains regular (the tempo does not change), the number of notes per beat continuously increases as the texture thickens and more instruments are introduced. In *Le Sacre du printemps*, rhythm is considerably more complex from the outset (to this fact we shall also return), growing increasingly more so as new melodic-rhythmic fragments are superimposed on its static harmony and as the texture becomes thicker, more active, and more varied in color.

The emphasis on color and texture in this music

is not confined to works for large orchestra. In Moussorgsky's *Pictures at an Exhibition* the sound possibilities of the piano, alone, are exploited seemingly without limits. How does Moussorgsky make the piano sound like, for example, chickens, an oxcart, an old witch, and even the great gate of Kiev? This wonderfully imaginative and unfettered use of the instrument for creating "sound pictures" stems from the following devices: (1) exploiting the suggestiveness of the various registers of the piano (high and low); (2) the use, at times, of a small, pinched range contrasted with a large, sweeping range at others; (3) contrasting all kinds of textures —thick chords, unison, thin linear textures; (4) demanding legato, staccato, or an almost percussive touch; (5) the use of rhythm to imitate, at times almost to mimic, the movement of the object depicted—for example, two Jews or children play-

*Victor Hartmann's Project
for the City Gate of Kiev
(Pictures at an Exhibition)*

*Victor Hartmann's Bronze Clock
in the Form of Baba Yaga's Hut
(Pictures at an Exhibition)*

ing; (6) and finally, the use again of particular combinations of tones (chords), not operating functionally but imitating and thus evoking images of people or things.

We have attributed the special quality of Russian music in part to the nationalistic loyalties of its composers. But to the folk-like melodies and the harmonic and structural characteristics which follow from them, must be added a particular kind of originality, stemming perhaps from the fact that all but one of the Mighty Five were amateurs who had had little formal musical training. Moussorgsky, in particular, was proud of being a self-taught composer; undoubtedly this was a crucial factor in his own peculiarly original style. All of Moussorgsky's music is in some way motivated by extra-musical considerations (he wrote no symphonies, no chamber music, no sonata forms), but how different it is from the music of Mahler, Strauss, or Wagner! The following comments written in a

Style and Music
History

letter to a friend express Moussorgsky's attitude toward academic music and learned musicians:[13]

In one [music school] Z . . and T . . , in their professorial, antimusical togas, stuff the heads of their students with various abominations and infect them in advance. The poor pupils see before them not human beings but two fixed pillars to which are nailed some silly scrawls said to contain the laws of music. . . . Being raised to the rank of a doctor of music—*a cobbler in an academic fool's cap*—he [Z . .] is not so childish as to base his opinions and advice on esthetics and musical logic—oh no! He has learned the rules and uses this as a smallpox antitoxin to inoculate against free learning anyone who longs to study art.

Moussorgsky was often criticized for his lack of "technique." Of this he says:[14]

Why do I, *do not tell me,* when I listen to our musical brethren, seldom hear a vital idea, but mostly stuff from a school-room bench—technique and musical ABC's? . . . Maybe I'm afraid of technique, because I'm poor at it? However, there are some who will stand up for me in art. . . .

. . . leave aside the boundaries of art—I believe in them only very relatively, because *boundaries of art* in the religion of the artist, means *standing still.* . . . I've taken up the cross and with lifted head, bravely and happily, I shall go forth against *all sorts of things,* towards bright, strong and righteous aims, towards a genuine art that loves man, lives with his joys, his grief and his sufferings.

[13] Letter to Mili Balakirev, written April 28, 1862 in the village of Volok; in Leyda and Bertensson, eds. and trans., *The Musorgsky Reader,* p. 44.

[14] Letter to Vladimir Stasov, written July 13, 1872 in Petrograd; in *The Musorgsky Reader,* pp. 192–194.

The Historical
Context

230

Finally, here is what Debussy writes about Moussorgsky:[15]

He is unique and will remain so because his art is spontaneous and free from arid formulas. Never has a more refined sensibility been conveyed by such simple means; it is like the art of an enquiring savage discovering music step by step through his emotions. Nor is there ever a question of any particular form; at all events the form is so varied that by no possibility whatsoever can it be related to any established, one might say official, form since it depends on and is made up of successive, minute touches mysteriously linked together by means of an instinctive clairvoyance.

## IV

These comments provide a convenient link to the French music of this period. Debussy's admiration and sympathy for Moussorgsky's music is reflected in his own music—perhaps not so much by "influence" (although he knew the Russian's music well) as by "elective affinity." The importance given to color and texture—the immersion in direct, sensuous sound relationships, together with the organizing processes we have observed, identify the fundamental similarity between Russian and French music. Let us consider these similarities, as well as the differences, between the two bodies of music, more carefully now. Listen to the following works:

Debussy, *Prélude à l'Après-midi d'un Faune,* 1894
Debussy, *Iberia,* Parfums de la Nuit, 1906–1909
Ravel, *Rhapsodie espagnole,* Prélude à la Nuit, 1907

[15] Claude Debussy, *Monsieur Croche the Dilettante Hater,* N. Douglas, London, 1927, p. 35.

*Claude Debussy*

Debussy, *Préludes,* Book II, no. 1, 1910–1913
Ravel, orchestration of Moussorgsky's *Pictures at an Exhibition,* 1922

In the first four examples we hear again music characterized by a kind of animated, ebullient stasis. The means of animation, however, are different, more subtle, perhaps more refined: perfume rather than a coronation or a great gate. In Parfums de la Nuit from *Iberia* the stasis is quite literal—a single note is sustained while melodic fragments hover above and below it. We relish the sound of each instrument (often a solo woodwind) as it appears and disappears. The melodic fragments are wispy (in contrast to the folk melodies of Russian music), defined neither by clear tonal relationships nor by phrase structure. Rhythmically, events take place extremely slowly, pulse seems nonexistent, and we are encouraged to surround ourselves with the sonorities without concern for their extension in time. Contrast and movement are created by the introduction of new sounds (new chords, a thicker or more active texture, different instruments); but instead of a juxtaposition of events as in Russian music, there is a merging of one sound into the next. Harmonically, this music does not obstruct or negate tonality (as was true in Wagner and Schoenberg) but rather seems to absorb it, replacing it with a chordal sonority which is often repeated up or down a series of whole steps. Unlike Moussorgsky's, Debussy's chordal sonorities are sometimes nontriadic combinations of pitches. Thus they are less defined, more amorphous.

In Ravel's *Rhapsodie espagnole,* Prélude à la Nuit, a single *melodic* motive generates the sense of stasis. The varieties of sounds it acquires seem endless; the varieties of surroundings it assumes give the listener full opportunity to revel in sensory delight. It is like watching the reflection of a branch in the water: it never moves, but it is moving all the time; motion is contained within the limits of its confining shape.

In his piano prelude we hear Debussy exploiting the sonorous qualities of a single instrument. Like Moussorgsky in *Pictures at an Exhibition,* Debussy seems able to work magic in creating unique piano sounds. But his purpose is less literal, or perhaps less pictorial, than Moussorgsky's. Debussy makes more of sounds for their own sake; their associations are secondary and somehow more private.

In all these works we have little feeling of directed motion. Instead of a German walking tour punctuated by arrival at certain destinations, our experience is one of sitting quietly, deeply absorbing a single vista. Debussy wrote of his *Images:*[16]

The music of this piece has this about it: it is elusive, and consequently cannot be handled like a robust symphony which walks on all fours (sometimes on threes, but walks nevertheless).

Besides, I am more and more convinced that music is not, in essence, a thing which can be cast into a traditional and fixed form. It is made up of colors and rhythms.

Finally, listen to Ravel's orchestration of Moussorgsky's *Pictures at an Exhibition.* (The work is the result of a fascinating intertwining of personalities and media: An exhibition of watercolors and drawings of architecture by Moussorgsky's friend, Victor Hartmann, inspired a set of pieces for the piano; Ravel, inspired in turn by these pieces, composed an orchestral version.) As you listen to the work, consider the following questions: Why do you think Ravel was drawn to the possibilities of orchestrating this work? In what ways does the orchestration change the effect? Do you think Ravel has improved it? Which piece do you like better; which more effectively evokes the intended images? Does Ravel's style intrude on Moussorgsky's?

V

Debussy, *String Quartet in G Minor,* 1893
Ravel, *String Quartet in F Major,* 1902–1903

Debussy and Ravel each wrote one string quartet. Both are rather early works, Debussy's dating from his thirty-first year. It is difficult to describe this

[16]From a letter to Jacques Durand, September 3, 1907; quoted in Morgenstern, ed., *Composers on Music,* p. 329.

piece adequately in the terms we have been using. Consider the second movement, for example, marked Scherzo ("assez vif et bien rythmé"): its relationship to traditional scherzos is tenuous though revealing. In form the movement can be described as ABA', but this fact seems unimportant in the light of its unique inner processes. Harmonically it could again be described as static—one bass note is maintained throughout a large part of the A section. Yet it seems inappropriate to describe the harmony negatively as without motion. In the context of tonal harmony the implications of the term "static" (as used in Demonstration 10) are quite different, because harmony plays a different role in that style where syntax is largely defined or generated by harmonic functions. Listening to this movement we perceive the bass note as a dynamic element, a constant against which all the events of the piece take place but which (like any background) is itself affected by them. For example, there is a passage near the middle of the A section (*b* in the *a b + a'* structure within A) in which the bass note is not played. This is a moment of tension, of climax; resolution occurs with the return of the bass note. Another point of tension occurs at the end of A, when the cello, carrier of the constant, takes up the predominant melody and goes on to form a transition to the B section.

Equally "static" is the melody—a single two-measure figure which is also repeated almost continuously throughout the A section. But like the bass it is not heard as unchanging—it does, in fact, move about. It is played in the beginning by the viola; the violin takes it up in the second half (a'); and finally it is given to the cello. But more important, its surroundings vary to such a degree that it is only after listening analytically that we realize it remains literally unchanged for long stretches.

Coming up, now, to the surface of the work, we focus on what is actually most immediately perceived: the sparkling pizzicato upper strings. Moving through a large range, they enliven the piece by creating marvelous rhythmic shifts from the prevailing three-beat to two-beat groups, teasing the regularity of the repeated motive, the beat, and the phrase grouping. Toward the middle (*b*) of the first section, the pizzicato "ingredient" takes over. The sparkling surface seems to absorb the rest at this moment of tension; the two constants (bass note and motive) cease, and we are left suspended, to return to an altered norm in which the sound fabric is tipped over—the motive appearing on top, the pizzicato underneath.

To describe this as *a b* + *a*′ is certainly correct, but does this place the work in the tradition of eighteenth- and nineteenth-century German composition? Does it significantly contribute to an understanding of its style? How does form function in this work? This last question is a crucial one in our consideration of stylistic character.

What of the B section, whose themes (related to A) are elusive enough to make it difficult to say whether they are one or several? What of the passages which we hear as "waiting," but not so much because of their dominant harmonic implications as because of their thinner texture and relative cessation of activity? What *does* articulate structure in this work; what means does Debussy use to create stability, tension, and climax? Is there a sense of directed motion? These are some of the questions that must be answered in attempting to define or describe the style of this music. Debussy warned against this, however, in a letter to a musician who tried to describe his harmonic style:[17]

[17] Letter to René Lenormand, quoted in Austin, *Music in the 20th Century,* p. 19.

The Historical
Context

236

Think of all the inexpert hands that will utilize your study without discrimination, for the sole purpose of annihilating those charming butterflies which are already somewhat crumpled by your analysis.

Listen now to the Ravel quartet, written 10 years later. Compare the second movement (marked similarly to Debussy's, "assez vif—très rythmé") with that of Debussy. Notice, for example, that the ABA' structure is much more clearly articulated. The B section is much slower and has a distinctly contrasting character; the return of A is prepared by a long passage in which the motives of A appear in fragmentary fashion, finally emerging full-blown in the return (A'). The return itself is closer to the original A section than it is in the Debussy movement. Harmonically Ravel depends more on functional chord relationships; we hear, for example, clear tonic-dominant and tonic-subdominant progressions; the melodies are more diatonic (although they have modal aspects, like the lowered seventh degree in the otherwise A minor opening melody). There is a stronger sense of pulse and a clearer articulation of the phrase rhythm in Ravel's work. The feeling of static structure is not a pervasive one. While color and texture are certainly a source of variety and contrast, they seem to reinforce the other structural elements rather than being, themselves, the means of structural articulation. For all these reasons Ravel is often said to be more in the "classical tradition" than Debussy. But what does this say in the light of Ravel's use of that characteristic French shimmer, his cascading of sounds and rhythms in the final movement of the quartet, his own kind of "distortion" of functional harmony, which makes it really quite different from the form it takes in the hands of Brahms or Strauss?

Style and Music
History

237

VI

Let us leave these questions for you to examine, and turn for a moment to opera, and then to another group of pieces which unites Russian and French forces, namely, music of the ballet.

Debussy wrote one opera, *Pelléas et Mélisande,* using Maeterlinck's symbolist play as his literary source. Like *Tristan und Isolde,* this is essentially a love story, but at no point does it approach the heavy, hyperemotional atmosphere characteristic of Wagner's opera. Even at the moment of greatest emotional intensity—when Pelléas and Mélisande finally declare their love for one another—the atmosphere is one of understatement, of a tender,

*Scene from the First Performance*
*of* Tristan und Isolde, *1865*

quiet make-believe world of unreal children. Compare this with the lengthy scene in which Tristan and Isolde meet as lovers (they still have two more hours to consummate their love).

Wagner, *Tristan und Isolde*, Act II, scene 2, 1857–1859
Debussy, *Pelléas et Mélisande*, Act IV, scene 4, 1902

As you listen, notice the difference in the relationship between the voices and the orchestra. Rarely in the Debussy opera does the orchestra impinge on the vocal line; indeed, the orchestra is once again often static, sustaining one sonority while the voice hovers above it in recitative-like song. We can hardly speak of motives or development of motives or even of phrases; the texture is characteristically shimmering but inactive in the Wagnerian sense; harmonically, also, we feel little sense of directed tension, avoided cadences, or ambiguous chromaticism. Tension is created coloristically—by instrumentation, range, contrasts in density of texture, increase in rhythmic motion. Notice particularly the beautiful moment when Pelléas says, "Je t'aime" and Mélisande answers, after a breath of silence, "Je t'aime aussi" on one, unaccompanied note. We are gently led into a world that seems ephemeral, refined, dreamy, and sensuous rather than emotional.

Turning finally to the ballet, we come once again to Stravinsky, in whom our rather rapid sweeps through Russia and France converge. Stravinsky's three early ballets were commissioned by Sergei Diaghilev, whose Ballet Russe had its first season in Paris in 1909. This company was a vital force in Parisian artistic life for 20 years. Diaghilev, the director; Fokine, his choreographer; and Nijinsky, his chief dancer, all played a part in the inception and realization of Stravinsky's early ballets.

Style and Music
History

(Diaghilev also commissioned Ravel's *Daphnis et Chloé,* as well as other works by Debussy, Stravinsky, Satie, and Prokofiev.)

These three ballets are all based on Russian folklore. Listen to the following excerpts (some of which you have heard before), noting particularly the changes in style between the earlier and the later works, the reflections of earlier Russian composers (Stravinsky, in fact, studied with Rimsky-Korsakov), and the effect of Stravinsky's wider international musical experiences.

*Firebird Suite,* Introduction, Dance of King Kastchei, Finale, 1910
*Petrouchka,* Part I, Part III, 1911
*Le Sacre du printemps,* Introduction, Dance of the Adolescents, 1913

Stravinsky wrote *Firebird* in Paris working closely with Fokine, giving him the music bit by bit as he wrote it and attending all the rehearsals of the company. The effect of this close association is hard to estimate, but surely the very special character of the work derives in some measure from the immediacy and excitement of performance and from the interactions between choreographer, dancers, and composer.

In *Firebird* and *Petrouchka* we hear the beginnings of the style that came to fruition in *Le Sacre du printemps.* In all three works we hear the sectionalism of the earlier Russian composers, the use of folk song, the strong pulse, and the coloristic use of instruments to activate the "static" harmony. But these characteristics are already becoming transformed in *Firebird.* There is greater variety within the sections made possible by the materials themselves. The pulse cannot be taken for granted—it is alive, shifting, grouped, and regrouped. Rhythmic patterns are established only to be extended or broken apart, fragmented and put back together, while the folk-like melodic fragments are treated similarly. The orchestra is larger and is used with all the imagination and skill of the earlier Russian and French composers, but Stravinsky adds new sounds (instruments played in unusual ways), along with a new kind of "layered" effect in which instrumental colors are heard intertwining with one another to create a more complex texture. Harmonically, sections are static, but tonal implications remain; for instance, we hear a repeated bass figure (*ostinato*) composed of fifths, and also a relatively tonal melody from which the harmonic sonority seems to derive (the opening of Kastchei's dance, for example).

In *Petrouchka* the ostinato becomes more important as an organizing, stabilizing factor in an atmosphere in which sonorities have become more complex (less triadic), and the texture thicker and more active. Notice how the ostinato functions in the opening of Part I: it is not simply a bass figure, but rather a kind of bubbling sound in which it is difficult to pick out individual instruments or even specific durations. It forms an animated color over which melodic fragments, solo instruments, and rhythms are superimposed like flashes. Often stopping abruptly as if used up, one ostinato yields to another, creating strong contrast and sectional articulation. How does Stravinsky's use of a "background" differ from Debussy's in his quartet or in *Iberia?* Why is an ostinato rare in the works of Schoenberg?

Melodic repetition also has a new life in *Petrouchka* because the recurrence of an iteration is unpredictable and rarely literal—Stravinsky constantly alters the length of the melodic fragment. Thus the static quality of repetition is there and not there at the same time. The first bubbling ostinato stops suddenly, yielding to a chordal texture—a kind of congealing of the whole sonority—which then becomes the norm to be unpredictably manipulated. One thinks of Matisse and his myriad textures, juxtaposed to form a design in which the viewer continuously discovers new relationships.

In *Le Sacre du printemps* Stravinsky created a work equalled in importance only by *Pierrot lunaire* as a disruption of the musical status quo, generating an equally new but quite different world of musical possibility. Indeed, the works symbolize the two approaches to music whose adherents, in the years that followed, often opposed one another. Stravinsky himself was more understanding and appreciative of *Pierrot lunaire* than many of his followers:[18]

Whatever opinion one may hold about the music of Arnold Schoenberg (to take as an example a composer evolving along lines essentially different from mine, both aesthetically and technically), whose works have frequently given rise to violent reactions or ironic smiles—it is impossible for a self-respecting mind equipped with genuine musical culture not to feel that the composer of *Pierrot lunaire* is fully aware of what he is doing and that he is not trying to deceive anyone. He adopted the musical system that suited his needs and, within this system, he is perfectly consistent with himself, perfectly coherent.

Yet at the same time Stravinsky viewed the piece from his own vantage point, in terms of his concern

[18]Igor Stravinsky, *Poetics of Music,* Vintage Books, Random House, New York, 1956, p. 14.

*Stravinsky Rehearsing* Le Sacre du printemps
Drawing by Jean Cocteau
(SPADEM by French Reproduction Rights, Inc., New York)

with instrumentation and texture, as these create design:[19]

. . . the instrumental substance of *Pierrot lunaire* impressed me immensely. And by saying "instrumental" I mean not simply instrumentation of this music but the whole contrapuntal and polyphonic structure of this brilliant instrumental masterpiece.

Why is *Le Sacre* considered a revolutionary work? (This was, incidentally, a reaction Stravinsky did not appreciate—"I confess that I am completely insensitive to the prestige of revolution.") Consider the opening: the bassoon plays alone at the top of its range, sounding to some listeners as marvelously new and strange, and to others as badly distorted; the melody, based on a Lithuanian folk

[19] Igor Stravinsky and Robert Craft, *Conversations with Igor Stravinsky,* Doubleday, Garden City, N.Y., 1959, p. 79.

Style and Music
History

song, is characteristically repetitive—a small collection of pitches varied by a completely flexible rhythm. As instruments are added, they combine to form sonorities that are no longer triadic but are the result of layers of fragmented melody superimposed, held together and made comprehensible either by an ostinato or by the flashes of repeated melody. Juxtaposition of textures and melodic fragments still characterizes the structural motion, but now the juxtaposition is more abrupt, episodes are shorter, and motives appear, disappear, reappear unpredictably, recognizable but often in new garb (see D7.13).

In the Dance of the Adolescents the unique sound

*Stravinsky*
Drawing by Pablo Picasso
(SPADEM by French Reproduction Rights, Inc., New York)

The Historical
Context

244

is created by superimposing two functionally unrelated triadic chords. It is as if Stravinsky had compressed Moussorgsky's juxtaposed chords into one sound which is neither of them. The unifying sonority is all-pervasive here—more so than in Stravinsky's earlier work because the sound itself seizes and haunts the listener. We feel a strong pulse, but the beats are grouped so irregularly (through sudden accents) that it is not a background but an active ingredient in the compositional fabric, a vital force in the effect of earthy sensuousness. Stravinsky said of the work, "I saw in imagination a solemn pagan rite: sage elders, seated in a circle, watching a young girl dance herself to death. They were sacrificing her to propitiate the god of Spring." While the composer breaks up the sonority in various ways to create, at times, a linear ostinato, it seems never to disappear. And to it he adds such a variety of elements that it is small wonder that the piece left its first-night audience reeling—flashes of coloristic sound, fragments of folk-like tunes, instruments playing at the extremes of their ranges, rhythms clashing and abruptly shifting—can you imagine the dance itself? Certainly it was far different from the toe dancing, arabesques, and tutus of nineteenth-century ballet.

Pagan rites, the half-mad Nijinsky dancing in Paris, while the moon-struck Pierrot sang in Vienna and Berlin! Go back now and listen to *Pierrot lunaire* with its concentration of detail; its thin, polyphonic texture; and its brief, closed, organic forms in which development means evolution of a seminal motive. How different from Stravinsky's static structure, within which melodic fragments and fixed sonority undulate and revolve, but somehow create, in themselves, definition and limits. And how very different in mood!

VII

Stravinsky once said,[20]

The creator's function is to sift the elements he receives from her [imagination, fantasy], for human activity must impose limits upon itself. The more art is controlled, limited, worked over, the more it is free. . . . My freedom thus consists in my moving about within the narrow frame that I have assigned myself for each one of my undertakings. I shall go even farther: my freedom will be so much the greater and more meaningful the more narrowly I limit my field of action and the more I surround myself with obstacles. Whatever diminishes constraint diminishes strength. The more constraints one imposes, the more one frees one's self of the chains that shackle the spirit.

As we stand back and consider the vista of 1860 to 1913—Wagner and Moussorgsky to Schoenberg and Stravinsky—we may view it in terms of the changing notions of limits and freedom and their relative importance. In a crucial sense a composer's style is defined by the personal, often unconscious limits he imposes on possibility and within which he finds the freedom to express what is relevant to him. Historically, we can watch and listen to the ebb and flow of this relationship between freedom and limits: Wagner and Moussorgsky living by and espousing the concept of expansive freedom, each in a different way; Schoenberg and Stravinsky each searching for his own limits to contain and at the same time intensify expressiveness. To view a work historically, then, is to grasp in it this kind of interplay between innovation and tradition; if at the same time the listener can perceive the unique process and design of each work with a sense of direct personal experience, then he is truly practicing the art of listening.

[20] Stravinsky, *Poetics of Music,* pp. 66 and 68.

# Suggested Reading

Abraham, Gerald, *A Hundred Years of Music,* 3rd ed., Aldine, Chicago, 1964.

Austin, William A., *Music in the 20th Century,* Norton, New York, 1966.

Newlin, Dika, *Bruckner, Mahler and Schoenberg,* King's Crown Press, New York, 1947.

Perle, George, *Serial Composition and Atonality,* 2nd ed., University of California Press, Berkeley, Cal., 1968.

Schoenberg, Arnold, *Style and Idea,* Dika Newlin, trans. and ed., Philosophical Library, New York, 1950.

Slonimsky, Nicholas, *Music Since 1900,* Norton, New York, 1937.

Stravinsky, Igor, *Poetics of Music,* Vintage Books, Random House, New York, 1956.

Stravinsky, Igor, and Robert Craft, *Conversations with Igor Stravinsky,* Doubleday, Garden City, N.Y., 1959.

Stravinsky, Igor, and Robert Craft, *Dialogues and a Diary,* Doubleday, Garden City, N.Y., 1963.

Stravinsky, Igor, and Robert Craft, *Expositions and Developments,* Doubleday, Garden City, N.Y., 1962.

Stravinsky, Igor, and Robert Craft, *Memories and Commentaries,* Faber, London, 1960.

White, Eric W., *Stravinsky: The Composer and His Works,* University of California Press, Berkeley, Cal., 1966.

*Ma Jolie*
Pablo Picasso, 1911–1912
(Collection, The Museum of Modern Art, New York;
acquired through the Lillie P. Bliss Bequest)

# A CHRONOLOGY

## MEDIEVAL,
## c. 400 to c. 1400

The Medieval Period (Middle Ages) spans the era from the fall of the Roman Empire through the fourteenth century. It is sometimes divided into the Early Middle Ages (400 to 1100) and Later Middle Ages (1100 to 1400), or the Romanesque and Gothic Periods. The sources for music history, especially when compared to the sources for art or literature, are quite rare until the later period.

| Excerpt | Composer, Title | Date | Source |
|---|---|---|---|
| 1 | *Veni Creator Spiritus* (Gregorian Chant) | ? | D1.5, D5.6 |
| 2 | *Salve Regina* (Gregorian Chant) | ? | D6.24 |
| 3 | *Gaudete Populi* (Mozarabic Chant, Easter antiphon) | ? | D2.3, E3.4 |
| 4 | *Desconforté ai esté / Amas qui m'a* (motet) | 13th c. | D3.8, E1.3 |
| 5 | *Lamento di Tristano* (dance) | 14th c. | D6.20 |

These five examples served earlier in the book primarily to illustrate some aspects of texture and melody. All but one (the thirteenth-century motet) illustrate unaccompanied melody (monophony),

# A Chronology of Composers and Genres

## MEDIEVAL (*Middle Ages; c. 400 to c. 1400*)

Composers anonymous until later
  Middle Ages
**Leonin** (late twelfth century)
**Perotin** (c. 1200)
Guillaume de **Machaut** (c. 1300–1377)
Francesco **Landini** (1325–1397)

Chant
Organum
Conductus
Motet
Mass
Caccia

Madrigal
Ballata
Virelai
Ballade
Rondeau

## RENAISSANCE (*c. 1400 to c. 1600*)

John **Dunstable** (c. 1385–1453)
Guillaume **Dufay** (c. 1400–1474)
Johannes **Ockeghem** (c. 1430–1495)
Jacob **Obrecht** (1452–1505)
Heinrich **Isaac** (c. 1450–1517)
**Josquin** des Prez (c. 1450–1521)
Adrian **Willaert** (c. 1490–1562)
Giovanni Pierluigi **Palestrina** (c. 1525–1594)
Orlandus **Lassus** (1532–1594)
William **Byrd** (1543–1623)
Thomas **Morley** (1557–1602)
Orlando **Gibbons** (1583–1625)

Motet
Mass
Madrigal
Chanson
Canzona
Magnificat

Anthem
Ricercare
Fantasia
Toccata
Dance music

## BAROQUE (*c. 1600 to c. 1750*)

Giovanni **Gabrieli** (c. 1557–1612)
Claudio **Monteverdi** (1567–1643)
Girolamo **Frescobaldi** (1583–1643)
Heinrich **Schütz** (1585–1672)
Giacomo **Carissimi** (1605–1674)
Jean-Baptiste **Lully** (1632–1687)
Arcangelo **Corelli** (1653–1713)
Henry **Purcell** (c. 1659–1695)
Alessandro **Scarlatti** (1660–1725)
François **Couperin** (1668–1733)
Antonio **Vivaldi** (c. 1678–1741)
Jean-Philippe **Rameau** (1683–1764)
Johann Sebastian **Bach** (1685–1750)
Domenico **Scarlatti** (1685–1757)
George Frideric **Handel** (1685–1759)

Opera
Cantata
Prelude
Concerto
Overture
Oratorio

Passion
Fugue
Sonata
Suite
Chorale-
  prelude

## CLASSICAL (c. 1750 to c. 1827)

Christoph Willibald **Gluck** (1714–1787)
Carl Philipp Emanuel **Bach** (1714–1788)
Franz Josef **Haydn** (1732–1809)
Johann Christian **Bach** (1735–1782)
Wolfgang Amadeus **Mozart** (1756–1791)
Ludwig van **Beethoven** (1770–1827)

Sonata
Symphony
Opera
Concerto

String quartet
Oratorio
Mass

## ROMANTIC (c. 1827 to c. 1900)

Carl Maria von **Weber** (1786–1826)
Gioacchino **Rossini** (1792–1868)
Franz **Schubert** (1797–1828)
Hector **Berlioz** (1803–1869)
Felix **Mendelssohn** (1809–1847)
Robert **Schumann** (1810–1856)
Frederic **Chopin** (1810–1849)
Franz **Liszt** (1811–1886)
Richard **Wagner** (1813–1883)
Giuseppe **Verdi** (1813–1901)
Johannes **Brahms** (1833–1897)
Georges **Bizet** (1838–1875)
Modest **Moussorgsky** (1839–1881)
Peter Ilyitch **Tchaikovsky** (1840–1893)
Giacomo **Puccini** (1858–1924)
Gustav **Mahler** (1860–1911)

Sonata
Symphonic poem
String quartet
Étude
Song (lied)
Oratorio

Symphony
Concerto
Nocturne
Ballade
Opera
Ballet

## TWENTIETH CENTURY

Claude **Debussy** (1862–1918)
Richard **Strauss** (1864–1949)
Erik **Satie** (1866–1925)
Arnold **Schoenberg** (1874–1951)
Charles **Ives** (1874–1954)
Maurice **Ravel** (1875–1937)
Bela **Bartok** (1881–1945)
Igor **Stravinsky** (1882–    )
Anton **Webern** (1883–1945)
Alban **Berg** (1885–1935)
Edgard **Varèse** (1885–1965)
Serge **Prokofiev** (1891–1953)
Darius **Milhaud** (1892–    )
Paul **Hindemith** (1895–1963)
Roger **Sessions** (1896–    )
Aaron **Copland** (1900–    )
Elliot **Carter** (1908–    )
Pierre **Boulez** (1925–    )

Sonata
String quartet
Overture
Ballet
Symphony

Concerto
Opera
Oratorio
Electronic
music

which prevailed in the earlier period until the development of polyphony. In the motet we hear three completely independent parts: the top two each have a different secular text; the bottom part, moving more slowly, is a fragment of chant.

It will be observed that only a small number of voices or instruments was used. For a variety of reasons, most of the music that has come down to us (in manuscript only, of course) is sacred vocal music; thus the music that we know from this period is oriented to the human voice and restricted by its limitations.

## Suggested Listening

Chant: Roman (Gregorian), Gallican, Ambrosian, and Mozarabic. (These terms refer to Catholic Chant cultivated in different parts of Europe in the Early Middle Ages; Mozarabic Chant, such as Excerpt 3 above, comes from Spain.)
Secular monophony: Troubadour and Trouvère music; Adam de la Halle, *Le Jeu de Robin et Marion* (a musical play).
Liturgical drama: *The Play of Daniel, The Play of Herod.*
Twelfth-century polyphony: Leonin, *Viderunt omnes;* Perotin, *Sederunt principes, Alleluya nativitas* (organum of the School of Notre Dame of Paris).
Guillaume de Machaut, Mass and secular works (fourteenth century).
Francesco Landini, secular works (fourteenth century).

## Suggested Reading

Reese, Gustave, *Music in the Middle Ages,* Norton, New York, 1940. The most comprehensive, scholarly work in English on medieval music (soon to appear in a new edition).
Strunk, Oliver, *Source Readings in Music History,* Norton, New York, 1950, pp. 59–190. Translations of writings by theorists and composers from ancient Greece through the Romantic Period. The readings for each period are also available in separate paperbound volumes.

The Historical
Context

## RENAISSANCE,
## c. 1400 to c. 1600

The Renaissance, literally a "rebirth"—a new era as those at the time saw it—went for its inspiration back past the "Dark Ages" to the glories of the classical civilizations of Greece and Rome. At the same time man's life and culture became increasingly secularized by the development of humanism. The Renaissance was a period of expansion in every area—geographical, economic, scientific, and cultural. The arts flourished at the many courts throughout Europe. Though the impetus for the Renaissance came from Italy, paradoxically most of the greatest music of the period was the product of Franco-Flemish composers who traveled throughout Europe. The sense of the age as being new and important is well illustrated by the following statement, made in 1477 by the Flemish theorist and composer Johannes Tinctoris: "There does not exist a single piece of music, not composed within the last forty years, that is regarded by the learned as worth hearing."[1]

Almost all the Renaissance excerpts listed here were used earlier to illustrate various aspects of texture. Excerpts 2 and 4 showed imitation, and Excerpts 7 and 10 showed polyphony in which the parts are of equal importance. A rehearing of these examples will reveal immediately that Excerpts 7 and 10 are also characterized by initial imitation. Excerpt 3 occurred in Exercise 1 as an illustration of no textural change in the course of the excerpt; it too is characterized by an active polyphonic texture. Only in Excerpt 1 is there a sense of dominance by one part of the texture. Renaissance

[1] *Liber de arti contrapuncti,* quoted in Friedrich Blume, *Renaissance and Baroque Music,* Norton, New York, 1967, p. 15.

A Chronology

253

| Excerpt | Composer, Title | Date | Source |
|---|---|---|---|
| 1 | Binchois, *De plus en plus* | c. 1450 | E2.7 |
| 2 | A. Gabrieli, *Ricercare* | c. 1580 | E3.2 |
| 3 | Palestrina, *Missa In festis Apostolorum,* Agnus Dei | c. 1580 | E1.17 |
| 4 | Palestrina, *Missa In festis Aposto- lorum,* Kyrie | c. 1580 | E3.5, D7.5 |
| 5 | Palestrina, *Missa Aeterna Christi munera,* Sanctus | 1590 | AM, Ch. 5[a] |
| 6 | Morley, *O Grief, E'en on the Bud* | c. 1590 | D3.7 |
| 7 | Gibbons, *Fantasia a 2* | c. 1608 | D2.7 |
| 8 | Gibbons, *Fantasia a 4* | c. 1608 | AM, Ch. 2 |
| 9 | Gibbons, *The Silver Swan* | 1612 | D3.9 |
| 10 | Ward, *Upon a Bank with Roses* | 1613 | E1.6 |

[a]"AM" refers to Additional Materials. "AM, Ch. 5" indicates that the excerpt originally was given in the Additional Materials section of Chapter 5. This form of abbreviation is used throughout Chapter 9.

music in general was polyphonic but showed great textural variety. Excerpt 9 by Gibbons was cited as illustrating the "textural flux frequently found in music, utilizing both of the kinds of textures" illustrated by the polyphonic examples on the one hand and Excerpt 6 by Morley, in which "all the parts move generally together" (*homorhythm*), on the other.

All but one (Excerpt 1) of the seven vocal pieces were performed *a cappella,* that is, by voices alone. In Excerpt 1, a Burgundian chanson, we hear a solo voice with instruments performing the other parts; the piece might have been performed, however, entirely by voices or instruments, or even with instruments doubling the voices. The performance practice of the period was flexible, and composers did not indicate instrumentation. The Gabrieli piece (Excerpt 2), which also did not specify instrumentation, is performed on modern brass instruments.

The Historical
Context

Two of the Palestrina examples (Excerpts 4 and 5) were discussed earlier as illustrating the continuous structure generated by polyphony. The second one, in particular, was described in terms of its so-called sixteenth-century "motet style," in which the piece proceeds through successive "points of imitation" at each new line of text, the new imitation overlapping the cadence which concludes the previous "section."

Our ten examples hardly give a "complete" picture of Renaissance music: only one is from the fifteenth century, three are by Palestrina, and three are by Gibbons. Four are from the early seventeenth century (the late Renaissance in Elizabethan England). The reader is encouraged therefore to listen to as many works as possible from the following list.

## Suggested Listening

Dunstable, *Veni sancte Spiritus, O Rosa bella.*
Dufay, secular works, *Missa Se la face ay pale.*
Ockeghem, secular works, *Missa Prolationum, Missa Fors seulement.*
Obrecht, *Parce Domine* (motet), *Missa Fortuna desperata.*
Isaac, *Innsbruck ich muss dich lassen, Quis dabit capiti meo aquam.*
Josquin des Prez, secular works, *Missa Pange lingua,* motets.
Willaert, madrigals, instrumental ricercare.
Palestrina, *Missa Papae Marcelli, Stabat Mater* (motet).
Lassus, secular works, *Missa Puisque j'ay perdu, Tristis est anima mea* (motet).
Madrigals of Marenzio, Morley, Gesualdo, and Monteverdi.
Instrumental pieces for lute, organ, and virginals.

## Suggested Reading

Blume, Friedrich, *Renaissance and Baroque Music,* Norton, New York, 1967.

A Chronology

Reese, Gustave, *Music in the Renaissance,* Norton, New York, 1959. An exhaustive, scholarly study of the period; almost more of a bibliographical reference work than a readable survey of Renaissance music.

Strunk, Oliver, *Source Readings in Music History,* Norton, New York, 1950, pp. 193–359.

## BAROQUE,
## c. 1600 to c. 1750

The period from the first year of the seventeenth century until the death of J. S. Bach in 1750 is called, borrowing the term from art history, the Baroque Period. As is true of all chronological delimitations of an era, the beginning and ending dates are conveniences rather than precise moments of historical change. Aspects of the new Baroque style begin to appear before 1600, and, on the other hand, younger composers began to develop a new style during Bach's lifetime. Also, within this century and a half—the period from Monteverdi through Bach—there are so many significant changes and developments that writers have difficulty defining the period as one era.

The examples from this period heard previously can hardly be considered a representative sample, for more than half of them are by a single late-Baroque composer, Johann Sebastian Bach (1685–1750). The generalizations which follow, therefore, are applicable primarily to late Baroque music, and the reader should listen to works by the seventeenth-century composers listed in the Suggested Listening.

As can be seen in the list of excerpts, most of the Baroque examples which appeared earlier in the book illustrated varieties of texture (Demonstrations 2 and 3 and Exercise 1), continuous organization (Demonstration 7), and sequence and imitation (Exercise 3). Indeed a description of the primary

The Historical
Context

256

| Excerpt | Composer, Title | Date | Source |
|---|---|---|---|
| 1 | Caccini, Madrigal | 1602 | D2.10 |
| 2 | Froberger, *Toccata 2* | c. 1650 | D7.7 |
| 3 | Lully, *Armide*, overture | 1686 | AM, Ch. 5 |
| 4 | Purcell, *Dido and Aeneas*, Dido's Lament | 1689 | AM, Ch. 5 |
| 5 | Vivaldi, *Concerto Grosso*, Opus 3, no. 3 | c. 1712 | E3.6 |
| 6 | Vivaldi, *Concerto Grosso*, Opus 3, no. 6 | c. 1712 | D6.8 |
| 7 | Vivaldi, *Concerto Grosso*, Opus 3, no. 7 | c. 1712 | E3.1 |
| 8 | Vivaldi, *Concerto Grosso*, Opus 3, no. 11 | c. 1712 | E3.14 |
| 9 | Bach, *Cantata 21* | 1714 | E3.10; AM, Ch. 7 |
| 10 | Bach, *Cantata 31* | c. 1715 | E1.19, D5.23 |
| 11 | Bach, *Partita 2*, unaccompanied violin, gigue | c. 1720 | D2.2, D6.26 |
| 12 | Bach, *Suite 2*, unaccompanied cello, sarabande | c. 1720 | AM, Ch. 7 |
| 13 | Bach, *Violin Concerto in E Major* | c. 1720 | E2.3 |
| 14 | Bach, *Two-Part Invention in F Major*, no. 8 | c. 1720 | D7.6 |
| 15 | Bach, *Suite in B Minor* | c. 1721 | D3.14, E1.8, E1.12 |
| 16 | Bach, *Brandenburg Concerto 2* | c. 1721 | AM, Ch. 3 |
| 17 | Bach, *Brandenburg Concerto 5* | c. 1721 | E1.11, D4.5 |
| 18 | Bach, *Well-Tempered Clavier*, Book I, Prelude no. 2 | 1722 | E2.4, D13.2 |
| 19 | Bach, *Well-Tempered Clavier*, Book I, Prelude and Fugue no. 3 | 1722 | D13.3 |
| 20 | Bach, *St. John Passion* | 1723 | D3.6, E1.15 |
| 21 | Rameau, *Suite in E*, gigue no. 2 | 1724 | D7.8 |
| 22 | Bach, *St. Matthew Passion* | 1729 | D2.6; D3.5; AM, Ch. 3; D6.25; D7.12 |
| 23 | Bach, *Harpsichord Concerto in D Minor* | c. 1730 | D1.4, D2.4 |
| 24 | Handel, *Concerto Grosso*, Opus 3, no. 1 | c. 1734 | AM, Chs. 4, 5 |

characteristics of late Baroque music would tend to focus on these areas. Many of the examples illustrate late Baroque polyphony, in which the independence of the parts which existed in earlier periods yielded somewhat to a polarity between

A Chronology

the outer voices: the lowest part (the *basso continuo,* played by a keyboard instrument playing chords and a bass instrument) was combined contrapuntally with the top part within a tonal context.

The Bach two-part invention (Excerpt 14) served in Demonstration 7 to illustrate continuous organization, the polyphonic interrelationship of the two parts generating a nonperiodic structure in which caesurae (and "predictable" phrase lengths) occurred infrequently. This kind of "spinning out," unravelling, of the rhythmic and melodic movement can be heard in most of the pieces listed above. Contributing to this effect is the prominent use of sequence (as in Excerpts 5, 6, 7, and 11) functioning rhythmically, melodically, and harmonically in building up the structure. One also feels a very strong pulse which is not, however, obviously broken up into metrical units.

Also apparent in the list of excerpts is the high proportion of instrumental works, many more than in the earlier periods. In the Baroque Period instrumental music developed at a rapid pace, and many of the instrumental genres still in existence today originated in this period (the sonata, concerto, and overture, for example). An important factor in the development and flourishing of instrumental music was the establishment, toward the end of the seventeenth century, of major-minor tonality which enabled composers to create more extended structures without relying on a text.

Suggested
Listening

Cantata: Schütz, Bach.
Concerto: Corelli, Vivaldi, Bach, Handel.
Ensemble sonata: Corelli, Vivaldi, Bach, Handel.

The Historical
Context

Keyboard music: Frescobaldi, Froberger, Chambonnières, Couperin, Rameau, Bach, Handel, D. Scarlatti.
Opera: Monteverdi, Lully, Purcell, A. Scarlatti, Rameau, Handel.
Oratorio: Carissimi, Handel.
Overture: Lully, A. Scarlatti.
Passion: Bach.

## Suggested Reading

Bukofzer, Manfred, *Music in the Baroque Era,* Norton, New York, 1947. This is the most comprehensive study of the entire period; it includes a very large list of Baroque books on music.

Grout, Donald, *A Short History of Opera,* 2nd ed., Columbia, New York, 1965, pp. 1–215.

Newman, William S., *The Sonata in the Baroque Era,* The University of North Carolina Press, Chapel Hill, N.C., 1959.

Strunk, Oliver, *Source Readings in Music History,* Norton, New York, 1950, pp. 363–615.

## CLASSICAL,
## c. 1750 to c. 1827

As with all periods, the dates defining the Classical Period are almost impossible to fix; it is generally marked off by the dates of the deaths of two composers—Bach in 1750 at one end, and Beethoven in 1827 at the other. Aspects of the classical style in music roughly parallel "neo-classical" developments in the other arts, which were inspired by the classical civilizations of Greece and Rome. To oversimplify, the style might be described in terms of the predominance of form over content, reason over emotion, manner over matter. Music, however, through three great composers—Haydn, Mozart, and Beethoven, all born within a 40-year period—reached greater heights than the other arts, combining these general stylistic attributes with personal expressiveness and meaning.

A Chronology

| Excerpt | Composer, Title | Date | Source |
|---|---|---|---|
| 1 | Haydn, *Symphony 8* | c. 1761 | AM, Ch. 2 |
| 2 | Mozart, *Variations on "Ah, vous dirai-je, Maman,"* K. 265 | 1778 | D7.4 |
| 3 | Mozart, *Sonata for Piano in A,* K. 331 | 1778 | D6.1, E4.3, E4.4 |
| 4 | Mozart, *Sonata for Piano in F,* K. 332 | 1778 | AM, Ch. 5 |
| 5 | Mozart, *Quartet in G,* K. 387 | 1782 | E1.14, D5.22, D12.7, E5.13 |
| 6 | Mozart, *Horn Concerto 2,* K. 417 | 1783 | E1.5, E2.1 |
| 7 | Mozart, *Quartet in D Minor,* K. 421 | 1783 | E4.6, D10.15 |
| 8 | Mozart, *Duo for Violin and Viola,* K. 424 | 1783 | D2.9 |
| 9 | Haydn, *Symphony 88* | 1787 | D4.4, D5.1 |
| 10 | Mozart, *Eine kleine Nachtmusik,* K. 525 | 1787 | D4.3; AM, Ch. 4 |
| 11 | Mozart, *Don Giovanni,* duet | 1787 | D6.21; AM, Ch. 3 |
| 12 | Mozart, *Symphony 39,* K. 543 | 1788 | AM, Ch. 4 |
| 13 | Mozart, *Symphony 40,* K. 550 | 1788 | D6.12; D11.3; D12.1; D12.2; E5.5; E5.6; AM, Ch. 7 |
| 14 | Mozart, *The Magic Flute,* aria | 1791 | D6.10 |
| 15 | Haydn, *Symphony 94* | 1791 | E4.18 |
| 16 | Mozart, *German Dance,* K. 605, no. 1 | 1791 | D7.1; AM, Ch. 5; D11.1 |
| 17 | Haydn, *Trio in G* | 1791 | D7.9 |
| 18 | Mozart, *Requiem* | 1791 | AM, Ch. 7 |
| 19 | Haydn, *Symphony 96* | 1791 | E2.8 |
| 20 | Haydn, *Symphony 97* | 1792 | E3.12; E4.17; D9.1; D10.10; AM, Ch. 7 |
| 21 | Haydn, *Symphony 99* | 1793 | D1.7; AM, Ch. 4; D11.2 |
| 22 | Haydn, *Symphony 100* | 1794 | E4.19, D9.6 |
| 23 | Haydn, *Sonata for Piano in C* | c. 1794 | D6.9 |
| 24 | Beethoven, *Minuet in G* | 1795 | E4.16 |
| 25 | Beethoven, *Ländler* | 1798 | E4.14, E4.15 |
| 26 | Haydn, *The Creation* | 1798 | D10.12 |

The Historical
Context

| Excerpt | Composer, Title | Date | Source |
|---------|-----------------|------|--------|
| 27 | Beethoven, *Trio*, Opus 11 | 1798 | D2.8; AM, Ch. 2 |
| 28 | Beethoven, *Quartet*, Opus 18, no. 1 | 1799 | D4.7, D5.25, D11.4, D12.4–12.6, E5.1, E5.2, E5.4, E5.7, E5.8 |
| 29 | Beethoven, *Quartet*, Opus 18, no. 4 | 1799 | E5.9, E5.10 |
| 30 | Beethoven, *Septet*, Opus 20 | 1800 | E4.20 |
| 31 | Beethoven, *Sonata for Violin and Piano*, Opus 30, no. 2 | 1802 | E2.6, E5.3 |
| 32 | Beethoven, *Symphony 3* | 1803 | E1.10, E1.16, E1.21, D5.16, D5.21, D10.2 |
| 33 | Beethoven, *Quartet*, Opus 59, no. 3 | 1806 | E1.9 |
| 34 | Beethoven, *Symphony 4* | 1806 | E5.11, E5.12 |
| 35 | Beethoven, *Symphony 5* | 1808 | AM, Ch. 4 |
| 36 | Beethoven, *Egmont*, overture | 1809–1810 | D10.5 |
| 37 | Beethoven, *Symphony 7* | 1811–1812 | E1.4 |
| 38 | Beethoven, *Symphony 8* | 1811–1812 | D10.11 |
| 39 | Beethoven, *Symphony 9* | 1823 | D6.5, D12.3 |
| 40 | Beethoven, *Quartet, Grosse Fuge*, Opus 133 | 1825 | D10.14; AM, Ch. 7 |
| 41 | Beethoven, *Quartet*, Opus 131 | 1826 | AM, Ch. 4 |

A glance at this list of pieces shows that the examples occur in almost every demonstration and exercise, revealing the great diversity of the style—diversity in almost every dimension of music. One might say that this variety, this freedom, requires the strictness of form which we have found in this music; at the same time this wealth of possibilities makes the rigorous structure come alive as process. Recall, for example, how our explanations of fundamental musical procedures, as well as of sectional and continuous organization, fed into our discussion of sonata form in Chapter 7. Moreover, because of the clarity of the style and the variety of musical possibilities it utilizes, it is easier to isolate and demonstrate many of the facets of music in this style than in any other.

In Chapter 2 (Additional Materials and Ancillary Reading), aspects of the classical orchestra and its function in articulating musical events are discussed. Two Mozart dances provided the material for the discussion of the fundamentals of rhythm in Demonstration 4, and in Demonstration 7 another Mozart dance served as a model of sectional organization. The examples in Exercise 4 illustrating various aspects of harmony (major and minor modes, full and half cadences, chord progressions) came almost exclusively from the Classical Period.

Demonstration 11 set forth the notion of listening in terms of a norm—in that case a schema derived from the classical minuet. Perhaps the fundamental tenet of classical style is this establishment of norms (and consequently expectations), deviations from which become highly significant: The integrity of the theme is violated in development, the predominant homophonic texture yields to polyphony at crucial points in the structure, harmonic stability is broken by modulation, and even metrical regularity is upset by syncopation. The term "balance" took on great significance, as composers succeeded in integrating and coordinating all facets of music into a balanced, unified style. A reconsideration of Demonstrations 9, 11, and 12 at this point should make clear to the reader (listener) the essentials of classical style.

## Suggested Listening

The pieces above would constitute an excellent listening list for this period. There are, perhaps, two omissions: (1) a Beethoven piano sonata, and (2) some works by lesser masters. If time permits, it would be especially instructive to listen to works by composers other than the three greats in the list above—two sons of Bach, Johann Christian and Carl Phillip Emanuel; as well as Clementi, Boccherini, Cherubini, and Paisiello, to name only a few of the many good composers in this fertile period.

## Suggested Reading

There is no comprehensive work for this period comparable to the books by Gustave Reese and Manfred Bukofzer for the earlier periods. The following books, however, are enlightening in their particular areas.

Grout, Donald, *A Short History of Opera,* 2nd ed., Columbia, New York, 1965, pp. 215–314.
Newman, William S., *The Sonata in the Classic Era,* The University of North Carolina Press, Chapel Hill, N.C., 1963.
Strunk, Oliver, *Source Readings in Music History,* Norton, New York, 1950, pp. 619–740.

## ROMANTIC, c. 1827 to c. 1900

In the nineteenth century, music occupied a unique position. According to the writer-composer E. T. A. Hoffmann, music was *the* romantic art; during the period the critic Walter Pater wrote that "all art constantly aspires toward the condition of music." A period which witnessed the increasing interrelationship among the arts and among the artists themselves, the nineteenth century saw music push toward extremes in all its dimensions—dynamics, length, and emotional expression, to mention only the most obvious. It is a regrettable fact that the Romantic and Classical periods together provide the great majority of works in the standard concert repertory—regrettable certainly not because this music is inferior to that of any

A Chronology

| Excerpt | Composer, Title | Date | Source |
|---|---|---|---|
| 1 | Rossini, *La Scala di Seta,* overture | 1812 | D6.4 |
| 2 | Schubert, *Allegretto in C* | 1816 | E4.5 |
| 3 | Rossini, *La Gazza Ladra,* overture | 1817 | D10.3 |
| 4 | Schubert, *Die Schöne Müllerin,* Der Müller und der Bach | 1823 | D2.11 |
| 5 | Schubert, *Die Schöne Müllerin,* Ungeduld | 1823 | D6.14 |
| 6 | Schubert, *Die Schöne Müllerin,* Der Jäger | 1823 | E2.2 |
| 7 | Schubert, *Ländler,* Opus 171, no. 4 | 1823 | D7.3 |
| 8 | Schubert, *Impromptu,* Opus 90, no. 2 | c. 1827 | AM, Ch. 5 |
| 9 | Schubert, *Die Winterreise,* Frühlingsträume | 1827 | D6.22 |
| 10 | Schubert, *Die Winterreise,* Der Lindenbaum | 1827 | E4.7 |
| 11 | Schubert, *Piano Sonata in B-flat* | 1828 | E3.8 |
| 12 | Schubert, *Quintet in C,* Opus 163 | 1828 | D5.15, D10.7, D11.5 |
| 13 | Rossini, *William Tell,* overture | 1829 | D4.1, D5.3, D5.4 |
| 14 | Berlioz, *Symphonie fantastique* | 1830 | D5.18 |
| 15 | Mendelssohn, *Piano Concerto in G Minor* | 1831 | E3.9 |
| 16 | Mendelssohn, *Symphony 4* | 1833 | D11.6 |
| 17 | Chopin, *Preludes,* Opus 28 | 1838 | D3.1–3.4, E2.5, D7.2, D13.1 |
| 18 | Verdi, *La Traviata,* aria | 1853 | D3.10, E1.1 |
| 19 | Liszt, *Faust Symphony* | 1854 | D10.13; AM, Ch.7 |
| 20 | Bizet, *Symphony in C* | 1855 | E2.11, E3.17 |
| 21 | Wagner, *Tristan und Isolde* | 1857–1859 | D6.27; AM, Chs. 5, 7; Ch. 8 |

| Excerpt | Composer, Title | Date | Source |
|---------|-----------------|------|--------|
| 22 | Brahms, *Variations and Fugue on a Theme by Handel* | 1861 | AM, Ch. 7 |
| 23 | Moussorgsky, *Boris Godunov* | 1868–1872 | AM, Ch. 5; Ch. 8 |
| 24 | Brahms, *Alto Rhapsody* | 1869 | Ch. 8 |
| 25 | Borodin, *Prince Igor, Polovetsian Dances* | 1869–1887 | Ch. 8 |
| 26 | Moussorgsky, *Khovantchina* | 1873–1881 | D6.23; AM, Ch. 3; Ch. 8 |
| 27 | Moussorgsky, *Pictures at an Exhibition* | 1874 | Ch. 8 |
| 28 | Bizet, *Carmen* | 1875 | D4.6 |
| 29 | Tchaikovsky, *Marche slave* | 1876 | D5.13 |
| 30 | Tchaikovsky, *Francesca da Rimini* | 1877 | D5.17 |
| 31 | Brahms, *Rhapsodie*, Opus 79, no. 1 | 1879 | E3.3 |
| 32 | Brahms, *Symphony 3* | 1883 | D6.15; AM, Ch. 7; Ch. 8 |
| 33 | Mahler, *Songs of a Wayfarer* | 1883 | D3.11 |
| 34 | Verdi, *Otello* | 1887 | D10.6 |
| 35 | Rimsky-Korsakov, *Capriccio Espagnol* | 1887 | Ch. 8 |
| 36 | Mahler, *Symphony 1* | 1888 | D1.8, D5.24, D10.9, D11.7 |
| 37 | Richard Strauss, *Don Juan* | 1888 | Ch. 8 |
| 38 | Johann Strauss, *Emperor Waltz* | 1888 | D4.2 |
| 39 | Tchaikovsky, *Symphony 6* | 1893 | D5.12 |
| 40 | Debussy, *String Quartet* | 1893 | Ch. 8 |
| 41 | Debussy, *Prélude à l'Après-midi d'un Faune* | 1894 | E1.20, Ch. 8 |
| 42 | Richard Strauss, *Till Eulenspiegel* | 1895 | E3.7 |
| 43 | Sousa, *Stars and Stripes Forever* | 1896 | D5.11 |
| 44 | R. Strauss, *Ein Heldenleben* | 1898 | D6.3 |
| 45 | Schoenberg, *Transfigured Night* | 1899 | Ch. 8 |

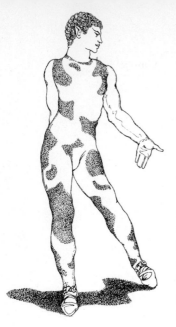

other period, but because in our time, for the first time in history, contemporary music does not constitute the bulk of the repertory.

The second half of the Romantic Period is treated in some detail in the model of procedure in the preceding chapter where eight of the twenty composers in this list are discussed. In this period color in harmony and instrumentation becomes a significant end in itself rather than a means to some structural end. (On the use of the orchestra in this respect see Chapter 2, Additional Materials and Ancillary Reading.) The piano, undergoing a number of technological improvements, was also exploited for its coloristic possibilities, and the orchestra grew in size with the addition of more and different winds (English horn, trombones, horns and trumpets with valves), harp, and many more percussion instruments.

Increasing chromaticism in harmony and changes in structural procedures were adumbrated in Demonstration 11 on the minuet and scherzo, and in the discussion of the first movement of Brahms' *Symphony 3* in the Additional Materials section of Chapter 7. It remains only to point out one more significant difference between this and music of earlier periods. Before the nineteenth century, composers often borrowed freely from preexistent musical sources—either their own works or the works of others. Thus style in these earlier periods is more generalized—there is a kind of community of composers and compositions within which the "beacons" of each era stand out. With Romanticism, the "art of the ego," individuality, becomes increasingly important and music (the theme especially) tends to take on the particular stamp of its composer.

The Historical
Context

## Suggested Listening

Ballet: Tchaikovsky.
Concerto: Mendelssohn, Schumann, Brahms, Liszt.
Opera: Verdi, Wagner, Moussorgsky, Puccini.
Oratorio: Berlioz, Liszt.
Piano music: Chopin, Liszt.
Quartet: Schubert, Brahms.
Sonata: Schubert, Brahms.
Song (Lied): Schubert, Schumann, Brahms, Wolf.
Symphonic poem: Liszt, Strauss.
Symphony: Schubert, Berlioz, Mendelssohn, Schumann, Brahms, Tchaikovsky, Mahler.

## Suggested Reading

Abraham, Gerald, *A Hundred Years of Music,* 3rd ed., Aldine, Chicago, 1964.

Einstein, Alfred, *Music in the Romantic Era,* Norton, New York, 1947.

Grout, Donald, *A Short History of Opera,* 2nd ed., Columbia, New York, 1965, pp. 315–493.

Strunk, Oliver, *Source Readings in Music History,* Norton, New York, 1950, pp. 743–902.

## TWENTIETH CENTURY

The Romantic and Modern Periods overlap, and in a sense the twentieth century proper did not begin until the second decade, while Romanticism lasted far into the century. The concern of advanced composers in the first decades of this century was to shake off the shackles of Romanticism, and the term "New Music" became a significant one. After World War II, electronic music and other aspects of the new technology became important musical factors.

The first thirteen years of the century, and six of

A Chronology

| Excerpt | Composer, Title | Date | Source |
|---|---|---|---|
| 1 | Schoenberg, *Gurrelieder* | 1901 | D10.1 |
| 2 | Mahler, *Kindertotenlieder* | 1901–1903 | D2.14 |
| 3 | Debussy, *Pelléas et Mélisande* | 1902 | Ch. 8 |
| 4 | Ravel, *String Quartet in F Major* | 1902–1903 | Ch. 8 |
| 5 | Debussy, *La Mer* | 1903–1905 | Ch. 8 |
| 6 | Ives, *Three Places in New England* | 1903–1914 | D3.15 |
| 7 | R. Strauss, *Salome* | 1905 | D3.12 |
| 8 | Schoenberg, *Chamber Symphony 1* | 1906 | Ch. 8 |
| 9 | Debussy, *Iberia* | 1906–1909 | Ch. 8 |
| 10 | Ravel, *Rhapsodie espagnole* | 1907 | Ch. 8 |
| 11 | Mahler, *Das Lied von der Erde* | 1908 | Ch. 8 |
| 12 | R. Strauss, *Elektra* | 1909 | Ch. 8 |
| 13 | Schoenberg, *Five Pieces for Orchestra* | 1909 | Ch. 8 |
| 14 | Ravel, *Daphnis et Chloé* | 1909–1912 | D5.2 |
| 15 | Schoenberg, *Quartet 2* | 1910 | Ch. 8 |
| 16 | Stravinsky, *Firebird Suite* | 1910 | E1.13; AM, Ch. 2; Ch. 8 |
| 17 | Debussy, *Préludes*, Book II | 1910–1913 | Ch. 8 |
| 18 | Schoenberg, *Herzgewächse* | 1911 | D1.6, D6.11 |
| 19 | Stravinsky, *Petrouchka* | 1911 | E2.9, Ch. 8 |
| 20 | Schoenberg, *Six Little Piano Pieces, Opus 19* | 1911 | D7.11; AM, Chs. 5, 7 |
| 21 | Schoenberg, *Pierrot lunaire* | 1912 | AM, Ch. 4; Ch. 8 |
| 22 | Webern, *Five Pieces for Orchestra* | 1913 | D1.9, E2.10 |
| 23 | Stravinsky, *Le Sacre du printemps* | 1913 | D1.3, D5.8, D5.9, D7.13, Ch. 8 |
| 24 | Berg, *Wozzeck* | 1915–1917 | D6.7 |
| 25 | Prokofiev, *Classical Symphony* | 1916–1917 | D6.18 |
| 26 | Milhaud, *La Création du monde* | 1923 | D6.19 |
| 27 | Stravinsky, *Octet for Wind Instruments* | 1923–1924 | D5.10, D6.13, E3.16 |
| 28 | Schoenberg, *Suite for Piano*, Opus 25 | 1925 | E3.13, D11.8 |
| 29 | Berg, *Lyric Suite* | 1925–1926 | D5.20 |
| 30 | Weill, *The Rise and Fall of the City of Mahagonny* | 1930 | E3.15 |
| 31 | Hindemith, *Mathis der Maler* | 1934 | E1.7, E3.11 |

| Excerpt | Composer, Title | Date | Source |
|---------|-----------------|------|--------|
| 32 | Webern, *Concerto for Nine Instruments* | 1934 | AM, Ch. 7 |
| 33 | Bartok, *Music for Strings, Percussion, and Celesta* | 1936 | D6.6; AM, Ch. 7 |
| 34 | Schoenberg, *Quartet 4* | 1936 | AM, Ch. 7 |
| 35 | Varèse, *Density 21.5* | 1936 | D2.1 |
| 36 | Bartok, *Sonata for Two Pianos and Percussion* | 1937 | D5.19; AM, Ch. 7 |
| 37 | Bartok, *Violin Concerto* | 1938 | D2.13 |
| 38 | Hindemith, *Ludus Tonalis* | 1942 | AM, Ch. 7 |
| 39 | Sessions, *Piano Sonata 2* | 1946 | AM, Ch. 7 |
| 40 | Boulez, *Le Marteau sans maître* | 1955 | D1.10, D3.13 |

the seventeen composers on this list (which is quite representative of the period before 1945), have been discussed at some length in the preceding chapter. It is nearly impossible, however, to give a cursory account of all developments during this century—partly because it has been a period of intensive experimentation, but mostly because the present is (perhaps refreshingly) without historical perspective.

In the early part of the century, rhythm awakened from its nineteenth-century torpor, and in a work such as Stravinsky's *Le Sacre du printemps,* it functioned, in a pseudo-primitive manner, as the primary material of the work. With the "emancipation of the dissonance" (see Chapter 8), the bonds of tonality became severely loosened (Excerpts 8, 12, and 19) or entirely broken (Excerpts 20, 21, 22, and 28). Of the early innovations (before 1945) the development of that means of organizing music called variously the *12-tone technique, dodecaphonism,* or more generally, *serialization,* by the Viennese group (Schoenberg, Berg, and Webern) seems to have been particularly fertile. Even Stravinsky in his later years (after 1957) adopted this method, although still maintaining his personal rhythmic and textural "gesture" (see, for example, his *Movements for Piano and Orchestra,* 1960, and *Threni,* 1958). Aaron Copland, who was influenced both by his years of study in France and by his American heritage, also incorporated the 12-tone approach in his work, for example, in his *Piano Fantasy* (1957).

Out of the original notion of serialization, which involved establishing an initial ordering of the 12 pitches which then became the normative "pitch set" for an entire work or at least one movement of a work, grew the possibility of ordering other aspects of music such as rhythm or timbre. Such music is described as "totally organized." Among composers following this direction, Milton Babbitt stands out as the leader and theorist in the American group.

At the same time other composers are writing what is known as *aleatoric* (*alea,* "chance") music in which one or more aspects are left (or only generally indicated) for the player to improvise in performance; that is, they are left to chance. John Cage has been a prime mover in this direction.

Composers have also put various electronic devices to work. In some instances a computer is programmed so as actually to "compose" music. (In this regard, the problems of devising the program as this activity relates to musical and stylistic analysis are particularly interesting.) In others, a composition, translated into a language of acoustic and durational components, is fed into an electronic synthesizer which produces the work directly on tape. The synthesizer does away with the necessity for live performance, thus exploding the limits previously imposed by instruments and human frailty.

But the human composer in his quest for personal expression must still make choices. Ultimately these choices involve a struggle between the challenge of possibility and the search for limits. "Well, of course the dialectic of freedom is unfathomable. . . ."[2]

## Suggested Listening

The works listed for the period constitute a representative group up to 1945 and should be heard in their entirety. In addition, other works by Stravinsky, Schoenberg, Webern, Berg, Ives, Bartok, and Varèse, as well as more recent music by composers such as Sessions, Carter, Dallapiccola, Copland, Boulez, Babbitt, and Berio should be studied.

## Suggested Reading

Austin, William A., *Music in the 20th Century,* Norton, New York, 1966. This is a thoughtful and very thorough book on the period, particularly the earlier years.
See, in addition, the bibliography at the end of Chapter 8.

[2]Thomas Mann, *Doctor Faustus,* Knopf, New York, 1948, p. 193.

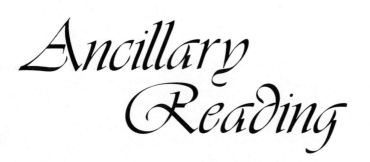
Ancillary Reading

## ACOUSTICS[1]

*Acoustics* is the science of sound. Sound, in music, consists in the impact on the ear of air vibrations set in motion by (1) the vibration of some elastic material, (2) the vibration of an air column in a pipe, or (3) vibrations electrically produced or transmitted. The elastic material may be (a) a gut string or wire, set in motion by a bow (violin), or plucked with the fingers (harp) or a plectrum (mandolin) or a quill (harpsichord), or hit with a metal tongue (clavichord) or a hammer (piano); (b) a reed or reeds set in motion by air pressure (oboe, clarinet); (c) a membrane set in motion by air pressure, such as the vocal cords (human voice) or the lips (brass instruments), or struck with a beater (drums); (d) a solid body, set in motion by striking (bells, triangle, xylophone).

The *intensity* of a note is determined by the amplitude of the vibration. Hence force is needed to produce a loud note.

The *pitch* of a note is determined by the frequency of the vibration. A low note vibrates slowly, a high one quickly. The frequency of the vibration may depend (1) on the length, thickness, tension, and density of the vibrating material, (2) on the length and density of the air column and the nature of the tube enclosing it, or (3) may be directly pro-

[1]Reprinted from J. A. Westrup and F. L. Harrison, eds., *New College Encyclopedia of Music*, Norton, New York, 1960, with the permission of William Collins Sons & Co., Ltd., Glasgow, Scotland.

duced by electrical processes. Thus, other things being equal, a short string will produce a higher note than a long one, a taut string a higher note than one less taut. A short air column will produce a higher note than a long one: the piccolo is shorter than the flute and so higher in pitch. On the other hand, the clarinet, though approximately the same length as the flute and oboe, is much lower in pitch than either. This is because it has a cylindrical tube stopped at one end (the mouthpiece), whereas the flute, though cylindrical, is open at both ends and the tube of the oboe, though stopped at one end, is conical or expanding. String and wind instruments are differently affected by temperature. A rise in temperature causes strings to expand, so that their tension is relaxed and they drop in pitch; but the expansion of air decreases its density, so that the pitch of wind instruments rises, the expansion of their material not being sufficient to counteract this.

The *resonance* of a note depends on the presence of some auxiliary material or an air column that will vibrate either in sympathy or by direct contact with the original vibrations. Thus the violin owes its resonance to its belly, the oboe to the air column contained in its tube. There is, however, an important difference. In the violin the belly has to vibrate as the strings dictate. In the oboe (as in other wind instruments) the vibrating air column, being of a definite length, controls the vibrations of the reed; so that in this case the resonator determines the pitch.

The *quality* of a note depends on the complex character of the vibrations. A stretched string does not merely vibrate as a whole. It also vibrates simultaneously in sections, which are in an exact mathematical relationship to the length of the string. These sections are the halves, thirds, quar-

Ancillary
Reading

ters, fifths and so on. The halves produce a note an octave higher than the note sounded by the whole string, the thirds a note a twelfth higher, the quarters a note two octaves higher, and so on. The "overtones" sounded by the respective sections fall into a series known as the *harmonic series*. If the principal note or "fundamental" is

the series will run as follows:

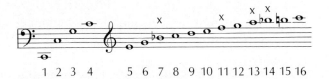

1  2  3  4      5  6  7  8  9  10 11 12 13 14 15 16

(The notes marked x are not in tune with our ordinary scale.)

The numbers of the series indicate exactly the mathematical relationship between the frequencies of the notes. Thus the ratio between:

and     is 1:2,

and     2:3,

and so on. The sound of the overtones is very much fainter than that of the note produced by the whole string, but without them the note heard by the listener would lose its lustre. The air column of a wind instrument or an organ pipe also vibrates in sections. If it is stopped at one end, as in some organ pipes, only alternate sections vibrate, so that a stopped pipe produces only Nos. 1, 3, 5, 7, etc.,

Chapter 2

277

of the harmonic series. Much the same thing happens with the clarinet, with its cylindrical tube stopped at one end. The characteristic tone-quality of instruments is thus due to the extent to which the "upper partials" (the overtones of the harmonic series) are present or absent and to their relative intensity. This makes it possible, in electronic instruments like the Hammond organ, to imitate closely the sound of orchestral instruments by presenting an artificial selection of the appropriate upper partials and giving to each the necessary intensity. In some instruments the overtones do not fall into the harmonic series and are therefore "inharmonic." The result may be a confused but recognizable sound, as in a bell, or one of indeterminate pitch, as in most percussion instruments.

By touching a string lightly at a point half-way from the end the player can prevent the whole string from vibrating while leaving the two halves free to vibrate. A similar result can be achieved by touching the string at other sectional points. The notes so produced are known, for obvious reasons, as *harmonics*. In the same way a wind-player, by increased lip-tension (known technically as "overblowing"), can split the air column in his instrument into one of its component parts, so that instead of sounding No. 1 of the harmonic series it produces one of the upper partials as its principal note. This is done to a limited degree on woodwind instruments and extensively on brass instruments. The horn, for example, has a choice of upper partials from the 2nd to the 16th harmonic. This explains why horn-players sometimes seem uncertain about their notes. The higher harmonics lie very close together, so that the selection of the right one by lip-tension calls for considerable skill. The extent to which members of the harmonic series are available on brass instruments depends

Ancillary
Reading

on the relation between the diameter of the tube
and its length. Neither the horn nor the trumpet,
being narrow-bored instruments, can sound No. 1
of the series.

## MUSICAL INSTRUMENTS

As we have maintained throughout this book, it
is your *experience* of music, rather than your intellectual grasp, that is primary. Thus in learning about
musical instruments, it is essential that you *hear*
various instruments to find out what they sound
like and what kinds of things they can do, separately and in combination. At this point, therefore,
you should listen to a recording of the instruments
of the orchestra. What follows here is a listing and
cursory discussion of musical instruments.

Note the final page of the score of *Symphony 1*
written in 1888 by Gustav Mahler and reproduced
on page 280. These 27 staves of music are played
by approximately 100 players constituting an orchestra similar in makeup if not in sound to that

*New York Philharmonic, Leonard Bernstein conducting*
(New York Philharmonic)

Chapter 2

in Debussy's *La Mer* (see the Additional Materials section of Chapter 2). At the left border of the page the names of the instruments are given and braces divide the staves into four groupings. These are the traditional divisions of the symphony orchestra: woodwinds, brasses, percussion, and strings.[2]

Woodwinds

Reading down from the top of the page, the woodwinds in the Mahler score are as follows: first and second *piccolos;* first and second *flutes;* four *oboes;* three *clarinets* in C, the fourth in E-flat; and three *bassoons* (called by the Italian term *fagotti*). According to the method of sound production and other factors, the woodwinds may be divided into three families, arranged from high to low within each family as follows:

*Flute.*   Piccolo, flute, alto flute, bass flute (rare).
*Clarinet.*   E-flat, B-flat, bass clarinet, double bass clarinet (rare); saxophones: soprano, alto, tenor, baritone, bass.
*Oboe.*   Oboe, English horn, bassoon, contrabassoon.

The *flute,* though classed among the woodwinds, is today usually constructed of metal. The player blows across a hole near the end of the instrument, causing a column of air to vibrate inside the tube.

The *piccolo* (Italian for "small") is literally a small flute; it is approximately one-half the size of the flute and consequently one octave higher in pitch.

[2]An all-encompassing scientific classification of instruments is as follows: *idiophones* (made of naturally sonorous material—instruments such as cymbals and chimes), *membranophones* (made of a stretched membrane, such as drums), *aerophones* (wind instruments), *chordophones* (strings), and *electrophones* (new electronic instruments such as the theremin or electronic organ.

Ancillary
Reading

*Flute, played by Julius Baker*
(New York Philharmonic)

The *oboe* is a double-reed instrument. The reeds
are made of cane. The player, inserting them into
his mouth, makes them vibrate against each other
by blowing.

The *English horn* (not used in the Mahler score)

*Piccolo, played by F. William Heim*
(New York Philharmonic)

Chapter 2

*Bassoon, played by Manuel Zegler*
(New York Philharmonic)

*Clarinet, played by Michael Burgio*
(New York Philharmonic)

Ancillary
Reading

is in effect an alto oboe, pitched a fifth below the oboe.

The *bassoon,* pitched approximately two octaves below the oboe, is also a double-reed instrument. In the Mahler score, the bassoons are written in the tenor clef (see Ancillary Reading, Chapter 4).

The *clarinet* has a single reed, which the player causes to vibrate against a slot in the pipe. Clarinets are what is known as "transposing instruments"; except when they are in C, they do not sound as written. In the Mahler score, the first three clarinets are in C, and like most other instruments, sound as written. The fourth clarinet in E-flat, however, sounds a minor third higher than written.

Brasses

The brass instruments in the Mahler symphony are seven (French) *horns,* four *trumpets,* first and second *trombones* (German, *Posaunen*), and third *trombone* and *tuba.* All these instruments are

*Trumpet, played by John Ware*
(New York Philharmonic)

Chapter 2

*French Horn, played
by James Chambers*
(New York Philharmonic)

*Trombone, played by Frank Crisafulli*
(Chicago Symphony Orchestra)

Ancillary
Reading

286

played by the players' lips vibrating in a mouthpiece inserted into the end of a folded metal tube
of some length. All except the trombone vary their
pitch by means of a combination of valves and
"overblowing" (increased tension of the lips). The
trombone uses a slide rather than valves.

Percussion

The percussion instruments shown in the Mahler
score are two *kettledrums* or *timpani* (German,
*Pauken,* here performed by two players), *triangle,*
cymbals (*Becken*), and *bass drum* (*Grosse
Trommel*). These are only some of a wide variety
of percussion instruments, which includes drums
of various sizes and kinds, gongs, castanets, wood
block, chimes, glockenspiel, tambourine, xylophone, and many more.

*Drums, played by Saul Goodman*
(New York Philharmonic)

*Violin, played by Frank Gullino*
(New York Philharmonic)

## Strings

The four principal strings are the *violin* (usually, as in the Mahler score, divided into first and second violins), *viola, cello* (full name *violoncello*), and *double bass* (so named because it frequently "doubled" the cello an octave lower)—also called *contrabass, bass fiddle,* or simply *bass.* These instruments all have four strings and are played most often with a bow (*arco*) or occasionally plucked (*pizzicato*).

As said previously, the orchestra playing the Mahler symphony would be composed of about 100 players: the 30 winds and 5 percussionists called for in the score, plus about 66 strings divided as follows: 18 first violins, 16 second violins, 12 violas, 10 cellos, and 10 basses. Thus, as can be seen, the strings constitute two-thirds of the orchestra, although they require only 5 of the 27 lines in this particular score.

Ancillary
Reading

*Cello, played by Asher Richman*
(New York Philharmonic)

*Double Bass, played by James V. Candido*
(New York Philharmonic)

Chapter 2

Compare the Mahler score with a page from the score of the *Symphony 8* by Joseph Haydn (c. 1761). The changes that occurred in the orchestra in a little over a century are apparent at a glance. The Haydn example illustrates the so-called "classical orchestra," with its nucleus of strings and a few added winds. During the nineteenth century, more and different winds and percussion were added, and many more players were added on each part in the string section.

A number of instruments have not been mentioned thus far. Instruments such as the organ, piano, harp, guitar, celesta, and vibraphone are not traditionally included among the regular components of the symphony orchestra, yet they are being utilized by composers more and more frequently today. In addition, there are the so-called "ancient"

*Harp, played by Edward Druzinsky* (Chicago Symphony Orchestra)

Ancillary
Reading

instruments, those which became obsolete at some point but which, either as originals or modern reconstructions, have been revived in the twentieth century: the families of viols and recorders, the harpsichord, clavichord, lute, cornetto, and shawm.

Finally, various smaller combinations of instruments, as they occur in *chamber music,* may be mentioned here:

*Trio.* *String* (violin, viola, cello) and *piano* (piano, violin, cello) trios are the most common.
*String quartet.* Two violins, viola, cello.
*Quintet.* *String* (two violins, two violas, cello; or two violins, viola, and two cellos), *piano* (piano and string quartet), or *woodwind* (flute, oboe, clarinet, bassoon, and horn).

## DYNAMICS AND EXPRESSION[3]

Dynamics

*Dynamics,* the relative loudness or softness (intensity) of musical tones, are indicated by markings derived from Italian. The basic signs are:

p    *piano,* soft
f    *forte,* loud

Modifications of these serve as very rough dynamic indications for the performer:

[3]In Medieval and Renaissance music there are no indications of dynamics and expression, but from the seventeenth to the nineteenth centuries they proliferate. It is in the "romantic" music of the nineteenth century and especially in contemporary music that we find the most detailed markings by composers.

Chapter 2

| | |
|---|---|
| pp | *pianissimo,* very soft |
| ppp | even softer |
| pppp | still softer |
| ff | *fortissimo,* very loud |
| fff | even louder |
| ffff | still louder |
| mp | *mezzo piano,* "half soft" (less soft than *piano*) |
| mf | *mezzo forte,* not so loud as *forte* |
| $<$ | *crescendo,* gradual increase in loudness |
| $>$ | *decrescendo, diminuendo,* gradual decrease in loudness |

Expression

Italian terms serve as indications to the performer of expressive shadings and character. Some of the more frequently encountered terms are listed below:

| | |
|---|---|
| *animato* | animated |
| *appassionato* | passionate |
| *cantabile* | in a singing style |
| *con brio* | with spirit |
| *con fuoco* | with fire |
| *con moto* | with movement (moving along) |
| *dolce* | sweet (soft) |
| *espressivo* | expressive |
| *grazioso* | graceful |
| *legato* | bound together, smoothly connected |
| *maestoso* | majestic |
| *marcato* | marked, emphatic |
| *pesante* | heavy |
| *sforzando (sf)* | forcing, that is, a single note strongly accented |
| *sostenuto* | sustained |
| *staccato* | detached, short |
| *tenuto* | held (the full value of the note) |

Ancillary
Reading

Obviously these indications of dynamics and expression, because of their vagueness, are subject to interpretation by the performer. For example, the term *appassionato* ("to be played in a 'passionate' manner") may have meant something specific to the composer, but it will of necessity mean different things to different performers. Thus the whole area of the interpretation and performance of music arises out of this terminological imprecision; and it is this which has led some composers recently to take their music into their own hands and out of those of the performer through electronic means.

## NOTES
## AND RESTS

Durational values are indicated by notes and rests which are related to each other in multiples of two. The rest, of course, means silence.

| | Whole | Half | Quarter | Eighth | Sixteenth | Thirty-second |
|---|---|---|---|---|---|---|
| NOTE | 𝅝 | 𝅗𝅥 | 𝅘𝅥 | 𝅘𝅥𝅮 | 𝅘𝅥𝅯 | 𝅘𝅥𝅰 |
| REST | 𝄻 | 𝄼 | 𝄽 | 𝄾 | 𝄿 | 𝅀 |

An indication of a *triplet* (3) alters the duple relationship among the notes. It is a direction to the performer to play three notes in the time usually taken by the two notes of the same value. Thus, 𝄽𝄽𝄽 = 𝄽𝄽 ; or, to put it paradoxically, $\frac{3}{8} = \frac{1}{4}$. That is, three notes are to be played in the time taken by one quarter note.[1]

A *dot* after a note increases its length by one-half its value.

𝅘𝅥. = 𝅘𝅥 + 𝅘𝅥𝅮 or 𝅘𝅥𝅮 𝅘𝅥𝅮 𝅘𝅥𝅮

A *tie*, 𝅘𝅥 𝅘𝅥 = 𝅗𝅥, connects two or more notes, indicating that the second note should not be sounded but that its duration should be tied to the first. It often occurs over a bar line, where the limitations of the measure make it impossible to write a half note.

[1] In addition to the triplet, the 2:1 ratio may be circumvented as follows:

⁵𝅘𝅥𝅮𝅘𝅥𝅮𝅘𝅥𝅮𝅘𝅥𝅮𝅘𝅥𝅮 = 𝅘𝅥𝅮𝅘𝅥𝅮𝅘𝅥𝅮𝅘𝅥𝅮 = 𝅘𝅥    ⁶𝅘𝅥𝅮𝅘𝅥𝅮𝅘𝅥𝅮𝅘𝅥𝅮𝅘𝅥𝅮𝅘𝅥𝅮 = 𝅘𝅥𝅮𝅘𝅥𝅮𝅘𝅥𝅮𝅘𝅥𝅮 = 𝅘𝅥    ⁷𝅘𝅥𝅮𝅘𝅥𝅮𝅘𝅥𝅮𝅘𝅥𝅮𝅘𝅥𝅮𝅘𝅥𝅮𝅘𝅥𝅮 = 𝅘𝅥𝅮𝅘𝅥𝅮𝅘𝅥𝅮𝅘𝅥𝅮 = 𝅘𝅥

Ancillary
Reading

Obviously, a note has no absolute length in itself. Its value is a function of the *tempo*. (Is the length of a quarter note 1 second, 3.8 seconds, or 0.75 seconds?)

## TEMPO
## DESIGNATION

While the metronome provides the only precise method of designating tempo (and therefore an absolute durational value for each note), most pieces are preceded by a verbal designation of the tempo in a most general sense. Once again, Italian terms predominate.

| | |
|---|---|
| *adagio* | slow |
| *largo* | very slow ("broad") |
| *andante* | moderately slow ("walking") |
| *moderato* | moderate |
| *allegretto* | moderately fast |
| *allegro* | fast ("cheerful") |
| *vivace* | fast ("lively") |
| *presto* | very fast |
| *prestissimo* | as fast as possible |

## TIME
## SIGNATURES

The time signature—expressed in a form much like a fraction—is placed at the beginning of a piece to tell us two things: (1) the meter, and (2) the durational unit of notation (that is, which notes will represent one beat). Thus in $\frac{2}{4}$ the upper number, 2, means that the piece is in duple meter, or to put it differently, that beats are grouped by twos. This grouping is reflected in the division of the written music into measures, each of two beats' duration. The lower number, 4, means that each beat will be represented by a quarter note or its equivalent duration.

The lower number is always one of the available notes listed above, and therefore a multiple of two (2, 4, 8, 16, 32).

𝅗𝅥 ♩ ♪ 𝅘𝅥𝅯 𝅘𝅥𝅰

2   4   8   16   32

The most common time signatures are $\frac{2}{4}$, $\frac{3}{4}$, $\frac{4}{4}$ (or C), $\frac{3}{8}$, $\frac{6}{8}$, $\frac{9}{8}$, $\frac{12}{8}$, $\frac{2}{2}$ (or ¢), and $\frac{3}{2}$.

Chapter 4
Pitch and
Movement

## PITCH
## NOTATION

Due to the vagaries of historical development, only seven letters are used to represent the twelve tones employed in Western music. Thus the letters *A* through *G*, with the aid of *accidentals* [*sharps* (♯) and *flats* (♭)], provide names for these twelve tones. In addition to being named by letter (which does not indicate the octave), pitches are notated on a five-line *staff* (). A *clef* (Latin *clavis*, "key") provides the key to the staff, as follows:

𝄞 is a G, or treble clef. It fixes the G above Middle C.

𝄞 G
C

𝄡 is a C, either alto or tenor clef. It fixes Middle C. The alto clef is used principally by the viola, the tenor clef by the bassoon, cello, and trombone.

𝄢 is an F, or bass clef. It fixes the F below Middle C.

Here are the twelve tones:

A    A♯=B♭  B   C   C♯=D♭ D  D♯=E♭  E   F   F♯=G♭ G  G♯=A♭

Oddly enough, A♯ and B♭, for example, are the same tones; they are called *enharmonic* equivalents.[1]

## KEY
## SIGNATURES

In tonal music (music written in a particular key) the key is indicated at the beginning of a piece by means of accidentals which constitute the key signature. Thus 🎼♭ means that all the B's in the piece are flatted, and the piece is in either F Major or D minor; while 🎼♯ indicates G Major or E minor.

A so-called "circle of fifths" illustrates the 24 major and minor keys. Starting from C Major, the key of

[1] These equivalents derive from a system of tuning called "equal temperament," which became standardized during the eighteenth century. While it is imposed on the piano by its construction, and therefore on instruments playing with it, string instruments playing together in small groups (a string quartet, for example) may make fine adjustments in pitch so that B♭ in a certain context may be slightly lower than A♯.

Ancillary
Reading

no sharps or flats, each sharp added to the key signature raises the key by the interval of a fifth, each flat added lowers it by a fifth.

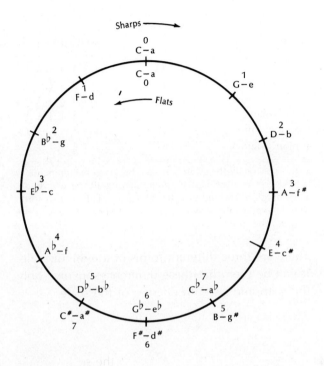

## MODES
## AND SCALES

The division of the octave into seven tones with different intervals between them creates the diatonic modes shown in the table on page 300.

The degrees of the scale in major and minor are named as follows:

1. Tonic
2. Supertonic
3. Mediant
4. Subdominant

5. Dominant
6. Submediant
7. Leading tone

| Name | Starting Note | Interval Pattern[a] |
|------|------|------|
| Dorian | D | 1 ½ 1 1 1 ½ 1 |
| Phrygian | E | ½ 1 1 1 ½ 1 1 |
| Lydian | F | 1 1 1 ½ 1 1 ½ |
| Mixolydian | G | 1 1 ½ 1 1 ½ 1 |
| Aeolian (minor) | A | 1 ½ 1 1 ½ 1 1 |
| Ionian (major) | C | 1 1 ½ 1 1 1 ½ |

[a] Thus playing all the white keys on the piano beginning on D would give you the Dorian mode; playing all the white keys beginning on E would give the Phrygian mode, and so forth. The interval pattern may be transposed to begin on any of the eleven other tones.

There are three different forms of the minor scale. It will be seen that these differences involve only the sixth and seventh degrees of the scale.

**Natural minor**

**Harmonic minor**

**Melodic minor**

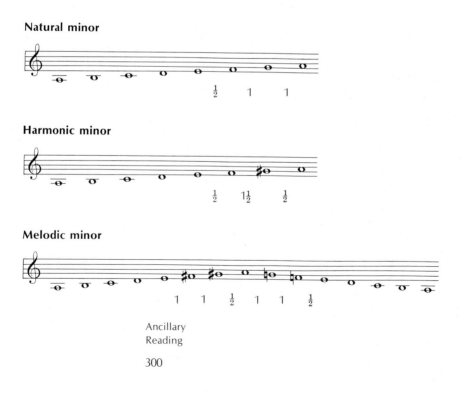

Ancillary
Reading

The harmonic minor is derived from the notes found in the I, IV, and V chords in their most common form (see the Ancillary Reading for Chapter 6, p. 303). The melodic minor is derived from ascending or descending melodies in the minor mode.

*The pentatonic mode.* The term *pentatonic* is used to describe various possible divisions of the octave into *five tones* (for example the black keys on the piano).

## INTERVALS

The distance between any two tones is called an interval. In discussing scales and modes, we spoke of a half step or a whole step; these may be more properly described as a minor second or a major second. The principal intervals within the octave are indicated below.

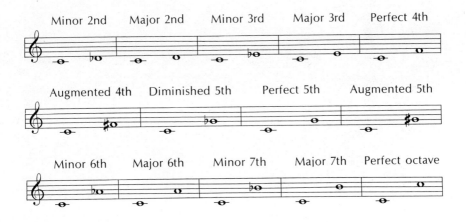

*Rules for naming intervals.* The *perfect* intervals are the *prime* (the same note), *fourth* ($2\frac{1}{2}$ steps), *fifth* ($3\frac{1}{2}$ steps), and *octave*. Lowering a perfect or a minor interval by $\frac{1}{2}$ step creates a *diminished* interval; lowering a major interval by $\frac{1}{2}$ step creates a *minor* interval. Raising a major or a perfect interval by $\frac{1}{2}$ step creates an *augmented* interval; raising a minor interval by $\frac{1}{2}$ step creates a *major interval.*

Ancillary
Reading

# Chapter 6

# Harmony

## THE BASIC
## TRIADS

The four basic triads are:

Major     Minor     Augmented  Diminished

root

In the course of time, additional thirds were added to the basic triads, creating sevenths, ninths, elevenths, and so forth:

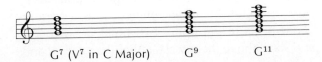

G⁷ (V⁷ in C Major)     G⁹     G¹¹

Triads can be built on each scale degree within a key; the following are the basic triads in C Major.

I     II     III     IV     V     VI     VII

The triads on I, IV, and V are major; II, III, and VI are minor; and VII is diminished.

Below are the basic triads in C minor.[1] The triads on V and VI are major; I and IV are minor; II and VII are diminished; and III is augmented.

I     II     III     IV     V     VI     VII

[1]The harmonic minor scale is derived from the practical use of these triads, particularly I, IV, V.

## INVERSION

There are a large number of possible arrangements of the notes of a chord. Below are four examples of a C Major triad. In the second example the root (C) is heavily "doubled." In the third, the triad is

played in *first inversion,* that is, with the third of the chord rather than the root in the bass. In the fourth example, the chord is in the *second inversion.* This chord is often referred to as a *six-four chord* because the upper two notes are a fourth and sixth above the lowest, rather than a third and fifth as they are in a root position triad.

## CADENCES

In the traditional study of harmony, chords are written in four parts. Various cadences are illustrated in the traditional manner.

Full (perfect, authentic) cadence    Half cadence    Plagal cadence    Deceptive cadence

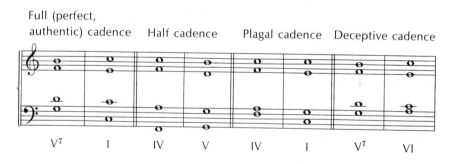

V⁷    I      IV    V      IV    I      V⁷    VI

Ancillary
Reading

304

# Glossary

The Glossary includes terms of a technical nature that have not been defined within the context of the discussion.

**Aria.** A song of some complexity, usually for one voice, with instrumental accompaniment. It occurs in operas, oratorios, and cantatas.

**Cadenza.** An improvisatory solo passage usually occurring near the end of a movement of a concerto where it serves to delay the conclusion and gives the soloist a chance to display his technical brilliance.

**Cantata.** Literally, a piece which is sung ("cantare"), in contrast to "sonata," a piece which is played ("sonare"). It is an extended choral work with or without solo voices and usually with orchestral accompaniment.

**Chorale.** A hymn tune of the German Protestant Church. These melodies are best known today through their harmonizations by J. S. Bach.

**Chromaticism.** The use of pitches in addition to those found in a given major or minor scale, therefore, a "mixing of families of pitches" (see p. 136).

**Coda.** Literally, "tail" (Italian); it is a passage at the end of a piece or movement which extends the ideas previously presented, bringing the work to a satisfying conclusion.

**Codetta.** A small coda, often occurring at the end of a section rather than at the end of a complete work.

**Concerto.** A work in several movements which exploits the contrast between a solo instrument and the full orchestra. A "violin concerto," for example, is a work for solo violin and orchestra; a "horn concerto" is a work for solo French horn and orchestra.

**Concerto grosso.** A work in several movements which exploits the contrast between a small group of solo instruments (called the *concertino*) and the full orchestra (called *tutti*).

**Countersubject.** A melody designed as a counterpoint to the subject of a fugue; it usually occurs for the first time above or below the second entrance of the subject.

**Deceptive cadence.** A cadence that sounds as if it were going to be conclusive until its final chord, at which point conclusion is interrupted (and the motion extended) usually by the substitution of the VI chord for I.

**Episode.** In the fugue, those phases in which the subject is absent or is present only in a fragmentary fashion (see p. 173).

**Fantasy, Fantasia.** A composition in which the composer "exercises his fancy"; thus, a work which tends to be freer in structure than one following a conventional form.

**Finale.** The last movement of an instrumental work written after about 1750, or the concluding section of an operatic act.

**First-movement form.** See sonata form.

**Flamenco.** Folk music of southern Spain (Andalusia).

**Fugue.** A polyphonic work in two or more parts built on a subject (theme) which is introduced in imitation and recurs frequently throughout the composition (see Chapter 7, pp. 171–181).

**Gavotte.** A French dance originating in the seventeenth century. It is in a moderate to fairly quick tempo and in duple meter (usually $\frac{4}{4}$ and often beginning on the third beat of the measure).

**Gigue.** One of the four traditional dance movements in suites written around 1700, usually the last (the standard movements being allemande, courante, sarabande, and gigue). It is characterized by compound meter and dotted rhythm, and frequently by imitative polyphony.

**Gregorian Chant.** The liturgical chant of the Roman Catholic Church, named after Pope Gregory I (590–604).

**Homophonic.** A texture in which one instrument (or voice) plays a dominant role while the other instruments play a clearly subordinate accompaniment (see Demonstrations 2 and 3).

**Impromptu.** A title given to a short piece for piano in the early Romantic Period.

**Interval.** The distance between two tones (see Chapter 4, Demonstration 6 and Ancillary Reading).

**Invention.** A term most commonly associated with a set of fifteen keyboard pieces by J. S. Bach which are written in two parts and are highly polyphonic.

**Ländler.** An Austrian dance in triple meter, forerunner of the waltz.

**Madrigal.** In the sixteenth century, a choral work, usually unaccompanied, with a text which the music follows rather closely. It is often imitative and polyphonic and tends to have a stronger sense of beat than its sacred counterpart, the motet.

**Mass.** A musical setting of the Roman Catholic service. Its major sections are: Kyrie, Gloria, Credo, Sanctus, and Agnus Dei.

**Metronome.** A device to indicate the precise tempo of a piece; invented by Mälzel in 1816 (see p. 36).

**Minuet.** A French dance of peasant origin in triple meter and moderate tempo. It had a great vogue at the court of Louis XIV.

**Motet.** A type of choral work, most often with a Latin sacred text, which had a long history in the Middle Ages and Renaissance.

**Movement.** The various self-contained sections of an extended instrumental composition such as a symphony, sonata, or string quartet.

**Mozarabic Chant.** The Catholic chant cultivated in Spain in the early Middle Ages.

**Ostinato.** A figure repeated persistently, often in the bass, while other elements of the texture change.

**Overture.** A term that most commonly refers to the instrumental music composed as an introduction to an opera, but also may refer to the first movement of a suite or to an entirely independent work (concert overture).

**Partita.** Originally (in the early seventeenth century) a term signifying a set of variations. In the late seventeenth century the term was also used to mean a suite.

**Passion.** A musical setting of the gospel accounts of the Passion (sufferings and death of Christ). In the seventeenth century it became a highly dramatic work for chorus and orchestra including recitatives, arias, chorales, and instrumental interludes.

**Polyphonic.** A texture in which instruments or voices move independently of one another and are all of relatively equal importance (see Demonstrations 2 and 3).

**Prelude.** Originally, an introductory movement in a suite or an introduction to another piece (as in a prelude and fugue). In the nineteenth century the term was used also as a title for individual piano pieces.

**Recitative.** A style of singing imitating and emphasizing the natural inflections of speech in both pitch and rhythm. It occurs in opera, oratorio, and cantata, and tends to serve a narrative function.

**Rhapsody.** A title given by composers in the nineteenth and early twentieth centuries to instrumental works of a somewhat heroic or "rhapsodic" character.

**Rondo.** Most often a movement in a larger work (symphony, sonata, or concerto—of which it is often the last movement) characterized by a highly sectional design which includes a recurring refrain alternating with contrasting material. It may be diagrammed as ABACADA. . . .

**Saeta.** A type of chant in Flamenco music improvised, usually by young girls, during the Good Friday procession.

**Sarabande.** A dance in slow triple meter which was one of the four dances included in suites around 1700.

**Scherzo.** Literally, "joke" (Italian); it is a movement in a symphony (or trio, quartet, or other instrumental work) taking the place of the minuet. Although faster in tempo, it is, like the minuet, in triple meter.

**Sonata.** Derived from the Italian *sonare* ("to sound"), it is a work in several movements for a small number of instruments.

**Sonata form.** A particular structural design found most frequently in the first movement of a sonata, symphony, or quartet, but also used in the slow movement and the final movement (see Chapter 7, Demonstration 12).

**Sonority.** The sound resulting from a particular combination of instruments, or (in late nineteenth- and twentieth-century music) the sound resulting from a particular combination of pitches.

**String quartet.** A group of four stringed instruments—two violins, viola, and cello; also, a work in three or four movements for these instruments.

**Suite.** Before approximately 1750 an instrumental composition consisting of several movements, each of them dance-like, and all in the same key; after 1750 a set of movements excerpted from a ballet or opera.

**Symphony.** Essentially a sonata for orchestra; that is, a work in several movements composed for a relatively large group of instruments.

**Theme and variations.** An independent work or a movement of a larger work (such as a sonata or symphony) in which a musical idea (theme) is presented and then varied so that some aspects of the theme remain constant while others undergo change. The composition is generally highly sectional and "additive" rather than developmental; each variation is often a self-contained unit.

**Timbre.** Tone color; that is, the quality of a tone as played by a particular instrument. Thus, the difference between tones of the same pitch when these are played by, for example, the violin or flute.

**Toccata.** From the Italian *toccare* ("to touch"), it is a composition for a keyboard instrument characterized by a free style, often with elaborate running passages contrasted with full chords, and occasionally containing fugal sections.

**Tone poem, or symphonic poem.** A nineteenth-century symphonic composition based on an extramusical idea that is either poetic or descriptive.

**Trio.** (1) A work for any three instruments. Thus, a "piano trio" is a composition for violin, cello, and piano; a "string trio" is usually a work for violin, viola, and cello; a "horn trio" may be a work for French horn, violin, and piano. (2) In the minuet or scherzo movement of a symphony, sonata, or quartet, the middle section played between the minuet or scherzo proper, and its repetition (see Demonstration 11).

**Variation.** See *Theme and variations*. In a more general sense variation consists in realizing the implications of any musical material as, for instance, in development.

**Waltz.** A dance in triple meter which may be slow or fast in tempo. It originated in the late eighteenth century in Austria, and stemmed from the Ländler or German dance.

# INDEX OF COMPOSERS AND WORKS

Index of Composers
and Works

Index of Composers
and Works

Symphony 40 (Mozart), 29, 68, 150, 153, 157, 168, 182, 199, 260
Symphony 88 (Haydn), 37, 41, 260
Symphony 94 (Haydn), 125, 260
Symphony 96 (Haydn), 91, 260
Symphony 97 (Haydn), 98, 125, 126, 135, 142, 143, 260
Symphony 99 (Haydn), 12, 81, 107, 108, 150, 151, 260
Symphony 100 (Haydn), 125, 129, 130–134, 260
Symphony in C (Bizet), 91, 99, 264

Tamil Folk Song, 18, 65
Tchaikovsky, Peter Ilyitch, 43, 44, 251, 265, 267
Telemann, Georg Philipp, 198
Three Places in New England, "Putnam's Camp" (Ives), 24, 268
Threni (Stravinsky), 270
Till Eulenspiegel (R. Strauss), 97, 265
Toccata 2 (Froberger), 103, 104, 194, 257
Transfigured Night (Schoenberg), 213, 265
Traviata, La (Verdi), 24, 28, 264
Trio, Opus 11 (Beethoven), 18, 31, 32, 261
Trio in G (Haydn), 103, 104, 260
Tristan und Isolde (Wagner), 75, 110, 194, 202, 206, 207, 225, 239, 264
Twinkle, Twinkle Little Star, 77, 80
Two-Part Invention in F Major, no. 8 (Bach), 103, 106, 107, 194, 257

Ungeduld (Schubert), see Schöne Müllerin, Die
Upon a Bank with Roses (Ward), 28, 254

Varèse, Edgard, 17, 251, 269, 271
Variations on "Ah, vous dirai-je, Maman" (Mozart), 102, 260
Variations and Fugue on a Theme by Handel (Brahms), 189, 265
Veni Creator Spiritus, 12, 42, 249
Verdi, Giuseppe, 24, 28, 141, 251, 264, 265, 267
Viderunt omnes (Leonin), 252
Vivaldi, Antonio, 51, 66, 67, 96, 97, 250, 257, 258

Wagner, Richard, 75, 110, 194, 202, 204, 205–210, 212, 239, 251, 264, 267
Ward, John, 28, 252
Weber, Carl Maria von, 251
Webern, Anton, 13, 91, 186, 216, 217, 251, 268, 269, 271
Weill, Kurt, 98, 268
Well-Tempered Clavier (Bach), 81, 90, 170, 178–181, 257
Willaert, Adrian, 250, 255
William Tell, overture (Rossini), 37, 41, 50, 264
Winterreise, Die (Schubert), 72, 124, 264
Wolf, Hugo, 267
Wozzeck (Berg), 66, 67, 268

# INDEX OF SUBJECTS

Index of
Subjects

Index of
Subjects